Telling the Dao
and Seeing the Wisdom

Telling the Dao and Seeing the Wisdom
©2024 Andre Iton/caroline booops sardine

Published by Hobo Jungle Press
St. Vincent & the Grenadines, W.I.
Sharon, Connecticut, USA

ISBN # 979-8-9897406-1-1
First edition
April 2024

All rights reserved. No part of this publication may be reproduced, distributed, or transmitted in any form or by any means, including photocopying, recording, or other electronic or mechanical methods, without the prior written permission of the publisher, except in the case of brief quotations embodied in critical reviews and certain other noncommercial uses permitted by copyright law.

Front Cover Art: Andre Iton
Back Cover Art: Caroline booops sardine

Telling the Dao and Seeing the Wisdom

Text by Andre Iton

Illustrations by caroline booops sardine

FOREWORD

The Dao, a Classical Chinese text, is a timeless gift to humanity written around 400 BC. Those who embrace its teaching will find it brings "timelessness" into the relative wisp of a human life. Its philosophy of action in accordance to the flow of Nature challenges us to unravel the veil of the intellect and open up to the reality of a boundless existence.

My first encounter with *The Dao* was in Japan in 1979. Standing in a bustling Kyoto book store, the English translation of the classical text found resonance in every cell of my Being, and became a treasured text that I would carry with me through the decades.

In reading Andre's interpretation of this powerful text, its resonance is by no means diluted. It journeys heart-in-heart with booops' drawings, gathering texture through meandering paths of infinite possibility.

This compilation transports us on a returning journey from one hemisphere to another and back again in an ever-uniting, evolving wisdom to process and ultimately transcend life's challenges.

Words and images synthesize as the visuo-verbal counterparts gently challenge us to surrender from grasping at societal dictates to look up into the Endless sky where All (or Nothing) will be revealed.

Andre and booops' creative partnership has manifested a supreme work from hearts of loving tenderness that can only be achieved through courageous surrender to the Eternal flow of life. That is Living the Dao.

Its beginnings may have been in the East, but *Telling the Dao and Seeing the Wisdom* entices us in the Caribbean islands to embrace our full imagination through multiple senses, bringing us into connection with our Nature legacy, the Source from which our Ancestors found true liberation in the Mystic realms of Creative Imagination. Just one of these pieces can provide a source of contemplation for a whole week. When revisited, it continues to resonate on new levels, spiraling our vibration ever-upward akin to a mantra or prayer.

Whatever perception or practice we bring to encounter this remarkable work, it will meet us where we are. From here or there it will carry us through words, image and perception as a complimentary symbiotic whole, permitting fresh insights necessary to re-discover ourselves as Boundless, Rising, Shining—as we were born to be.

From within our tiny-island shores, booops and Andre have gifted Us a universal work as timeless as *The Dao* itself.

Momoife
St. Vincent

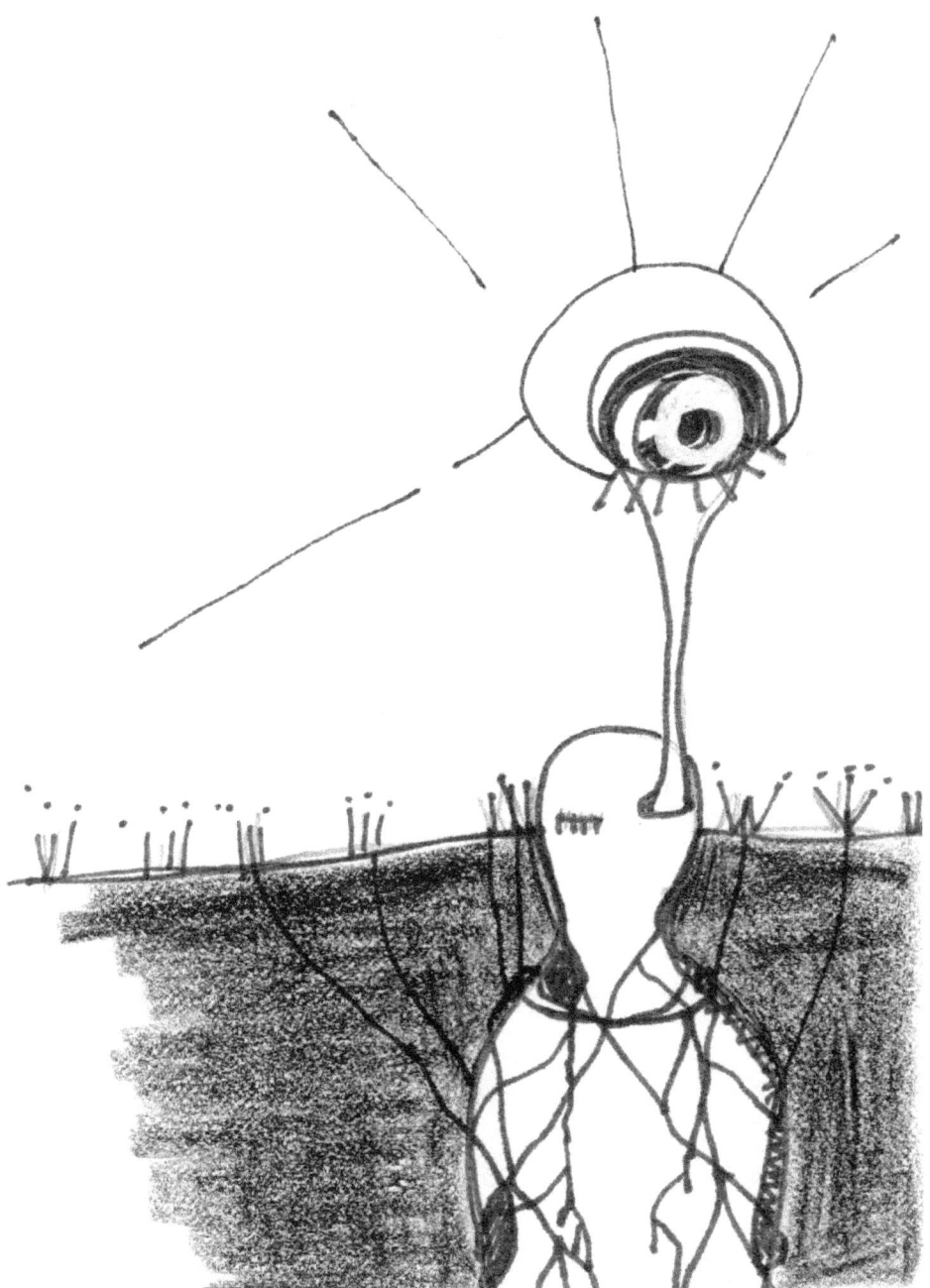

1.

The untold,
The unspoken,
The beginning,
The end,
The darkness.
The path to
Eternal Light.

2.

Beauty and Ugliness
Good and Evil
Riches and Poverty
Highs and Lows
Wins and Losses
Quiet and Noise
Peace and Wars.
For each to be manifest
The other must be.
For eternity
Nothing must be.

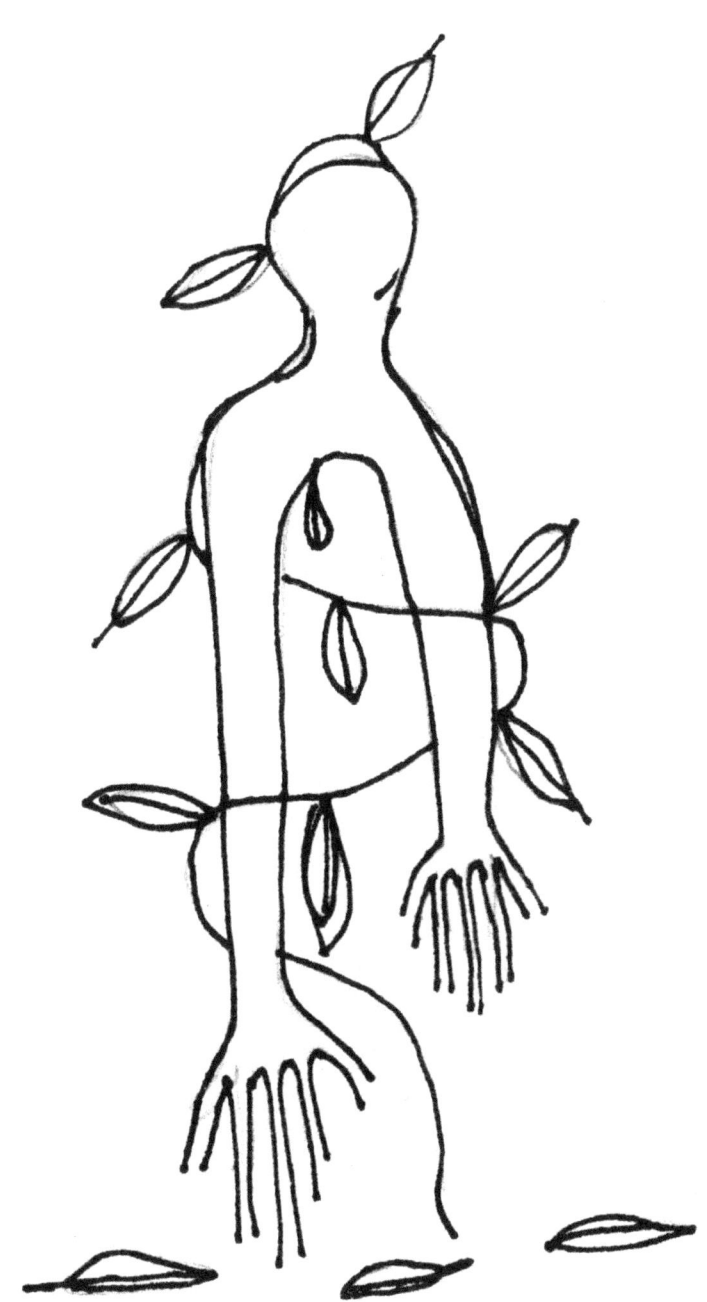

3.

With my feet on the ground
and my pace measured,
others can walk beside me.
Together, we can journey in harmony
With nature.
Together, we can learn that we know nothing
And that all we need to know is the Nothingness
that is the essence of all being.

4.

The Source of all existence
is unknowable.
It fills the rivers.
It parches the desert sands.
It fashions birth.
It decrees death.
It is knowable only
To its unknowable Self.

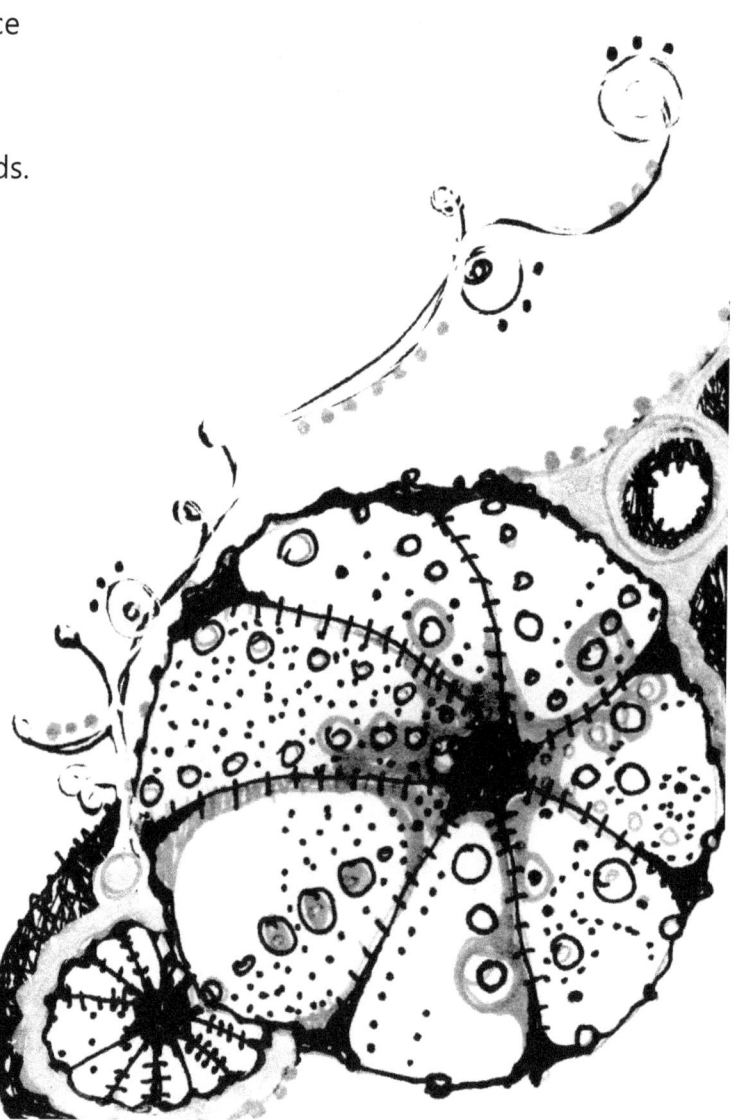

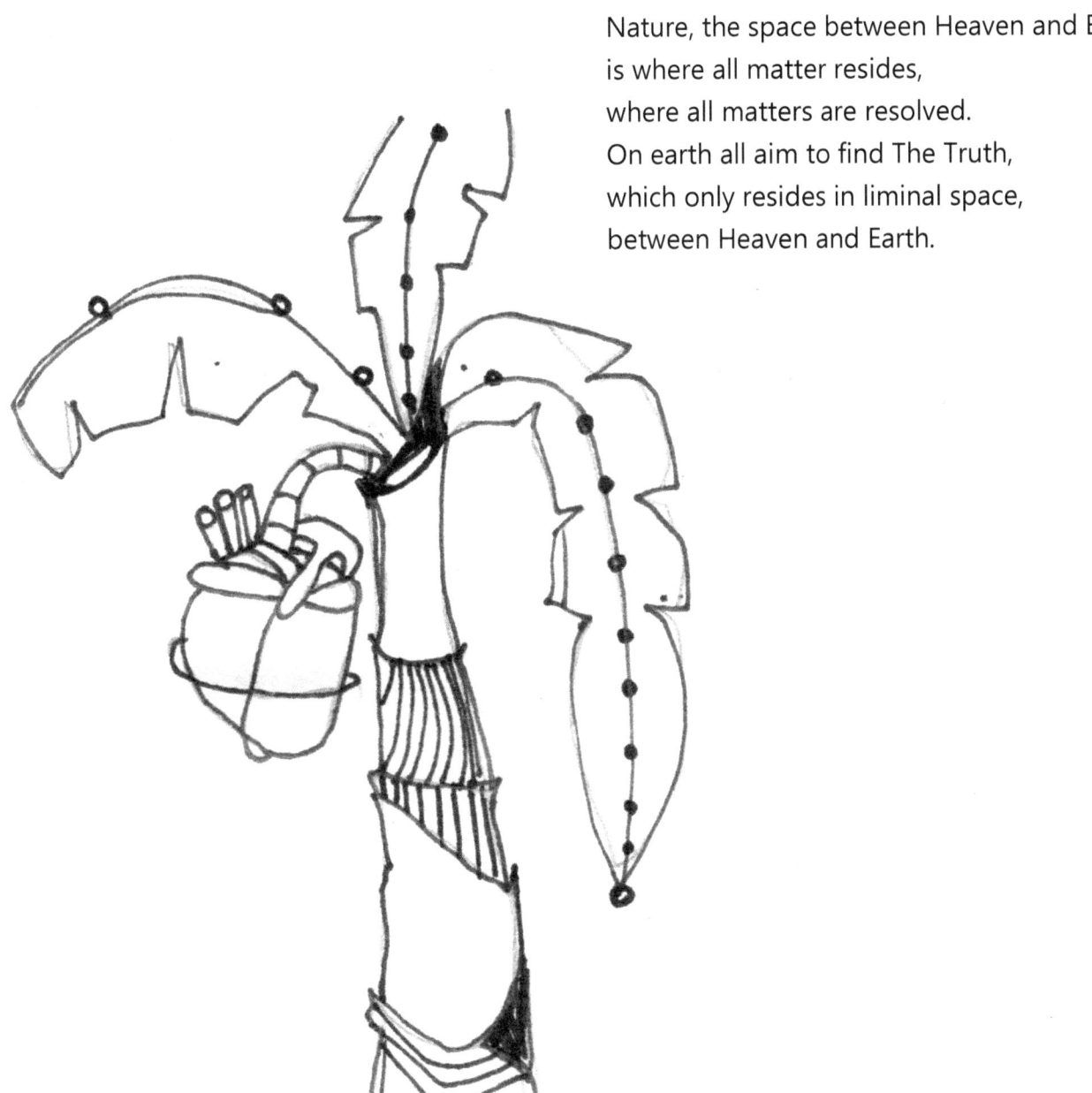

Nature, the space between Heaven and Earth
is where all matter resides,
where all matters are resolved.
On earth all aim to find The Truth,
which only resides in liminal space,
between Heaven and Earth.

6.

Life emerges,
through the portal,
Maternal.
Be ever mindful
of the need to treat both
with Grace.
Life,
delivered with maternal grace.
Given by the Eternal Unknown.

7.

To be born,
is the preparation
for Death.
Heaven and Earth
are unborn.
They prepare
for Life.
With wisdom,
The born
prepare for
Heaven and Earth.

8.

At The source
Water is pure.
It flows, with the capacity to cleanse itself.
It traverses the land,
gently, deeply and honestly,
never impairing nature.
On reaching the Sea,
it is greeted with great joy.
It surrenders.
to The Oneness of Eternal Water.

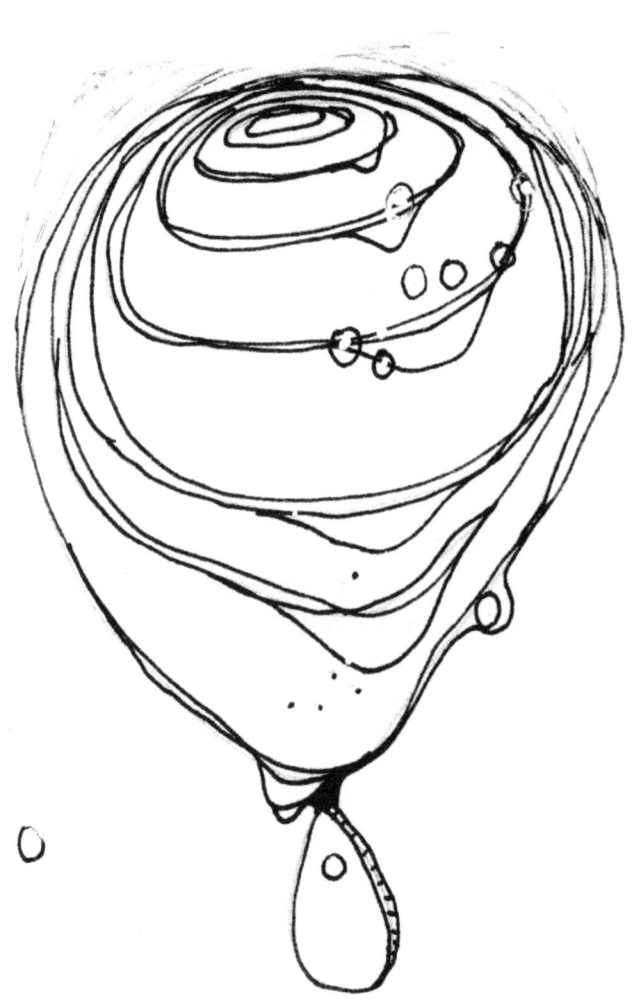

9.

To have enough is to know compassion.
To see enough is to have knowledge.
To feel enough is to have empathy.
To be enough is to know heaven.

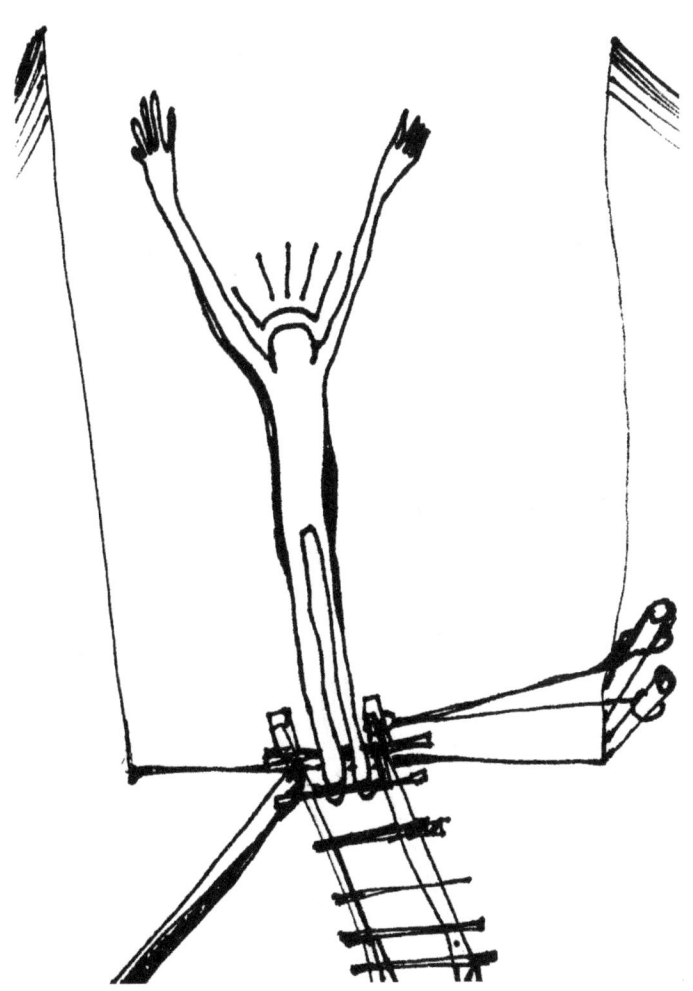

10.

Attend to the body
but do not neglect the soul.
Attend to the soul
but do not despise the body.
Seek ever the place where the body and soul
are in harmony.
For therein is complete union of all things.
From there you will see Heaven.

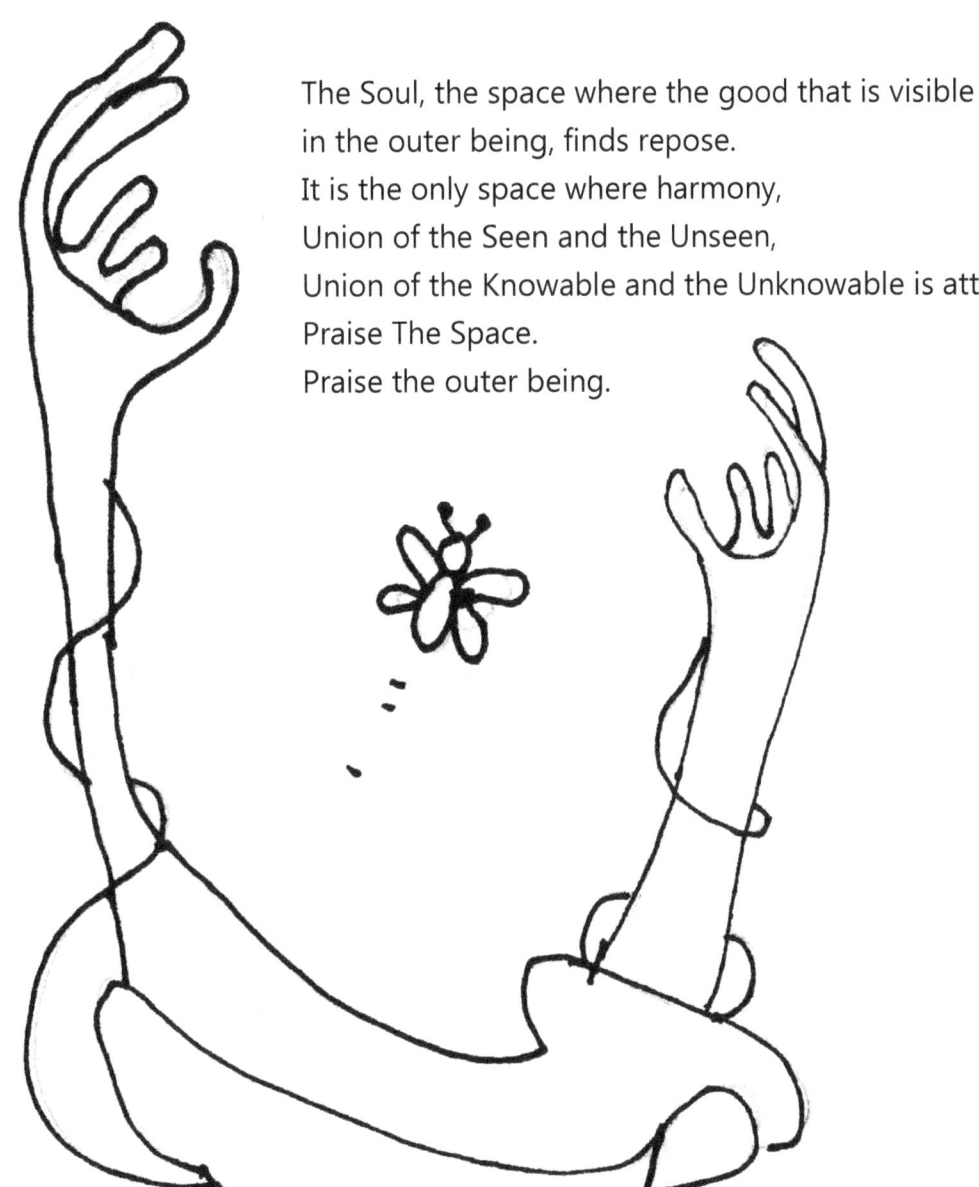

The Soul, the space where the good that is visible
in the outer being, finds repose.
It is the only space where harmony,
Union of the Seen and the Unseen,
Union of the Knowable and the Unknowable is attained.
Praise The Space.
Praise the outer being.

12.

Only that which one cannot see,
cannot touch
cannot hear
cannot feel
cannot smell
is real.
Only that,
lasts Forever.

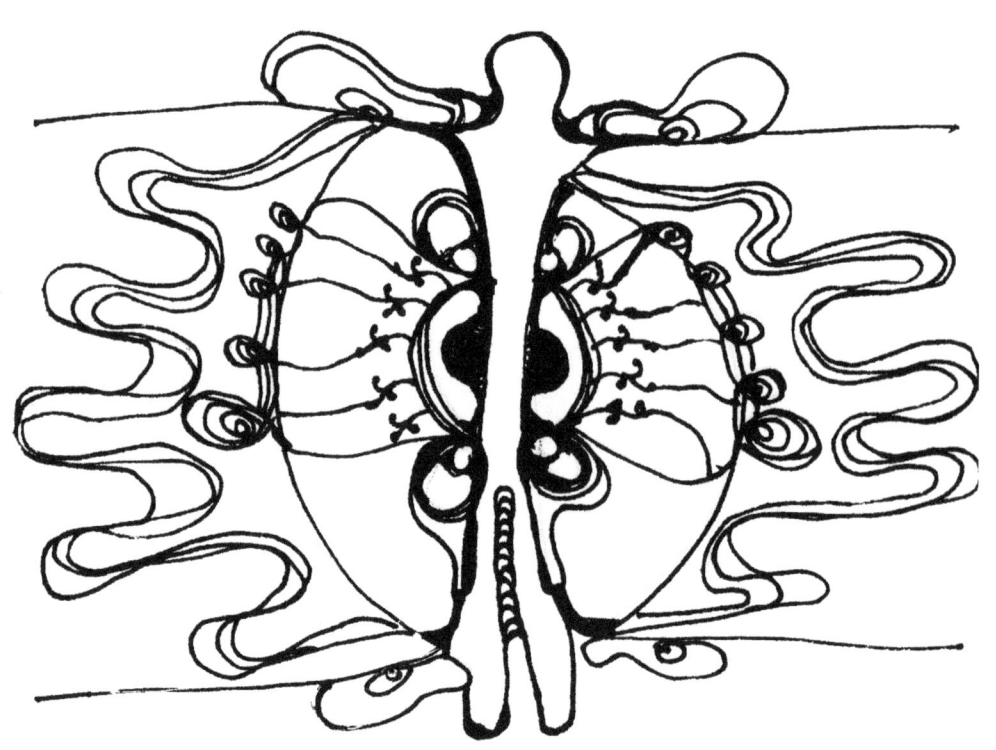

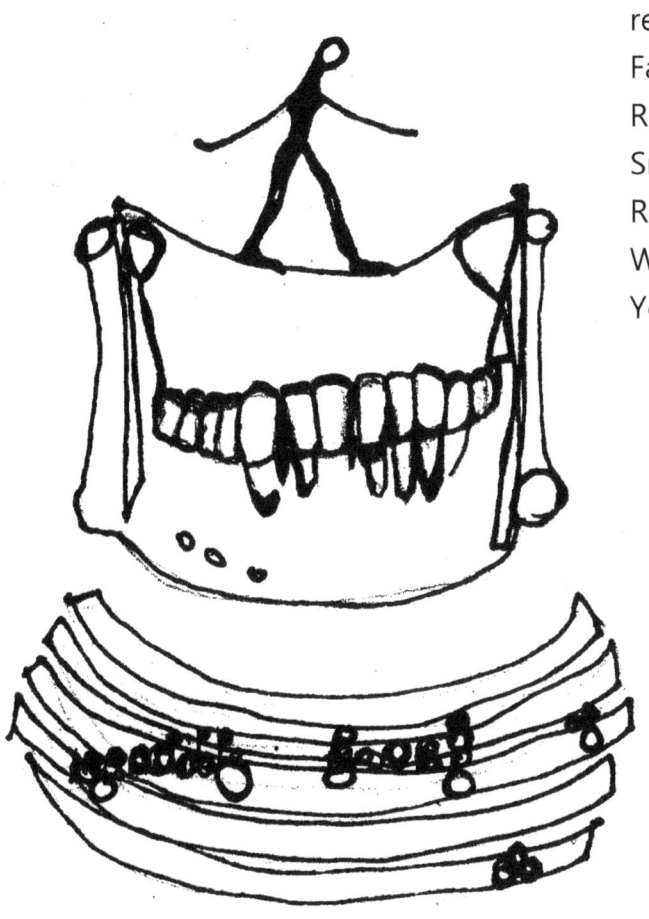

When the whole world laughs at you
smile gently.
When you fall,
recognize you are learning the art of balance.
Fall and Rise.
Rise and Fall.
Smile with grace in the face of ridicule.
Rise with praise after each fall.
With Grace, In Praise, you are Nature's own.
You are nothing but Heaven's child.

14

Unseen yet revealed.
Unspoken yet uttered.
Untouched yet joined.
To Eternity.
Revealed by the Heavens.
Spoken by the winds.
Touched by the seas.
The Heavens
The winds
The seas
The Revelations of The Eternity we seek.

15.

To know that the mystery of life,
the essence of being, is unknowable,
is the prerequisite for a peaceful existence.
To know that one does not know.
leaves space for all to unfold,
as The Source ordains.
Unfolding as ordained,
one flows gently to The Source.

In contemplation,
The mind is at peace.
It is emptied, yet acutely aware of the essence of life.
Breath.
Breath
a gift from The Source
   given generously, to all the living.
   Breath, in its absence,
   the living unites with The Source,
   for Eternity.

17.

That which is known can be loved or hated.
That which is unknown can be revered or feared.
Those who trust can expect trust.
Those who love can be known or unknown.
Knowing or Unknowing,
in silence, with love,
we find communion.

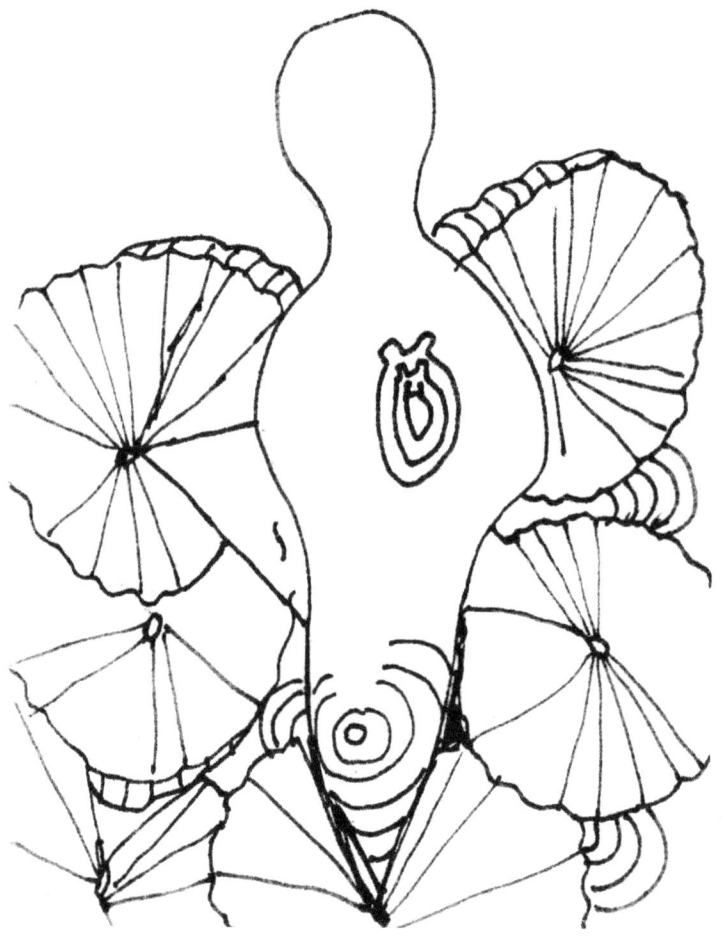

Innocence begets kindness and morality.
With wisdom and intelligence, pomposity abounds.
Familial conflict adjures fealty.
Societal chaos adjures truly patriotic leadership.

19.

Where there is love
there is little need to pursue perfection.
There is little need to seek to accumulate knowledge and wealth.
Where there is love
there is union with nature.
Where there is love
The sole desire of the self is to be selfless.

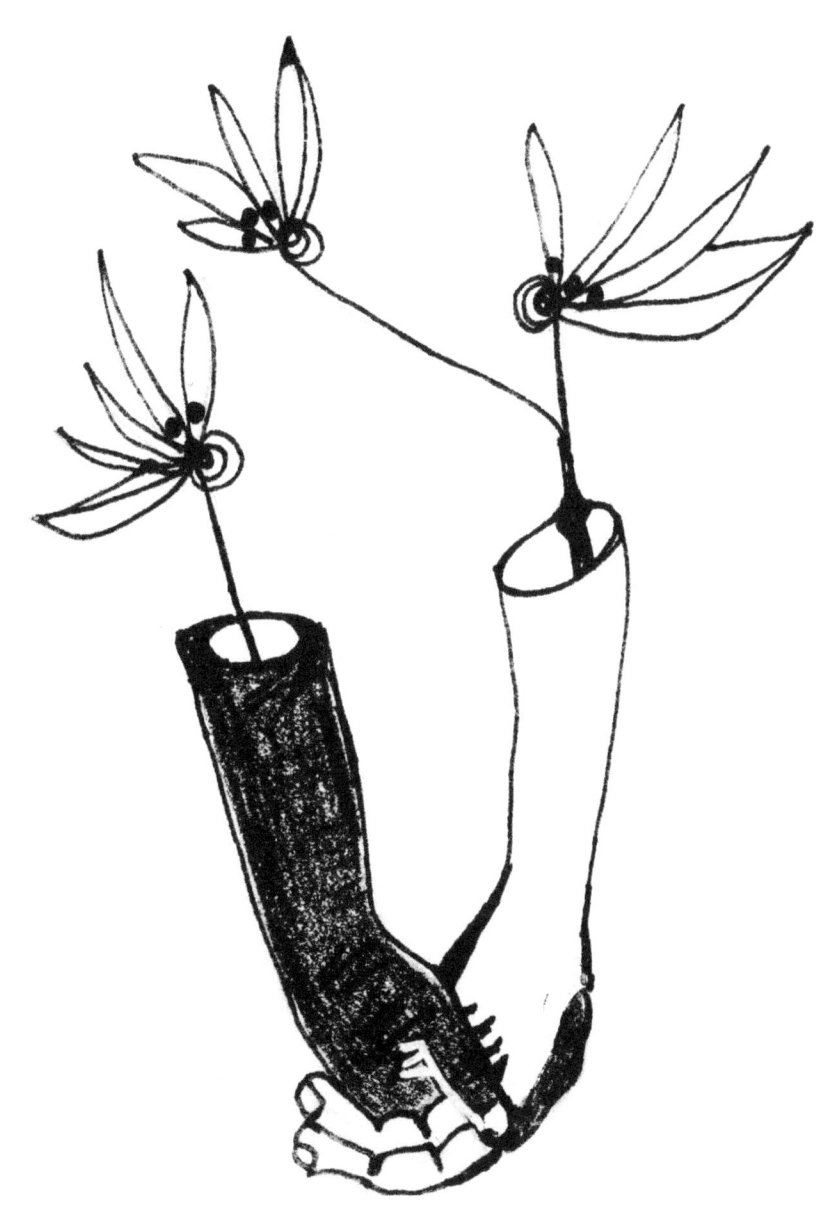

20.

In the pursuit of knowledge,
I am terrified by my lack of knowledge.
In the pursuit of good,
I am terrified by my capacity for evil.
In the pursuit of wealth,
I am terrified by my fear of poverty.
Observing others,
I am terrified by my capacity for envy.
Looking at the world,
I am confused and dejected.
Looking outwards,
I am always invisible to the world.
Looking inwards,
I am illuminated by my connection to The Source.
Looking inward, I am in the embrace of the Eternal.

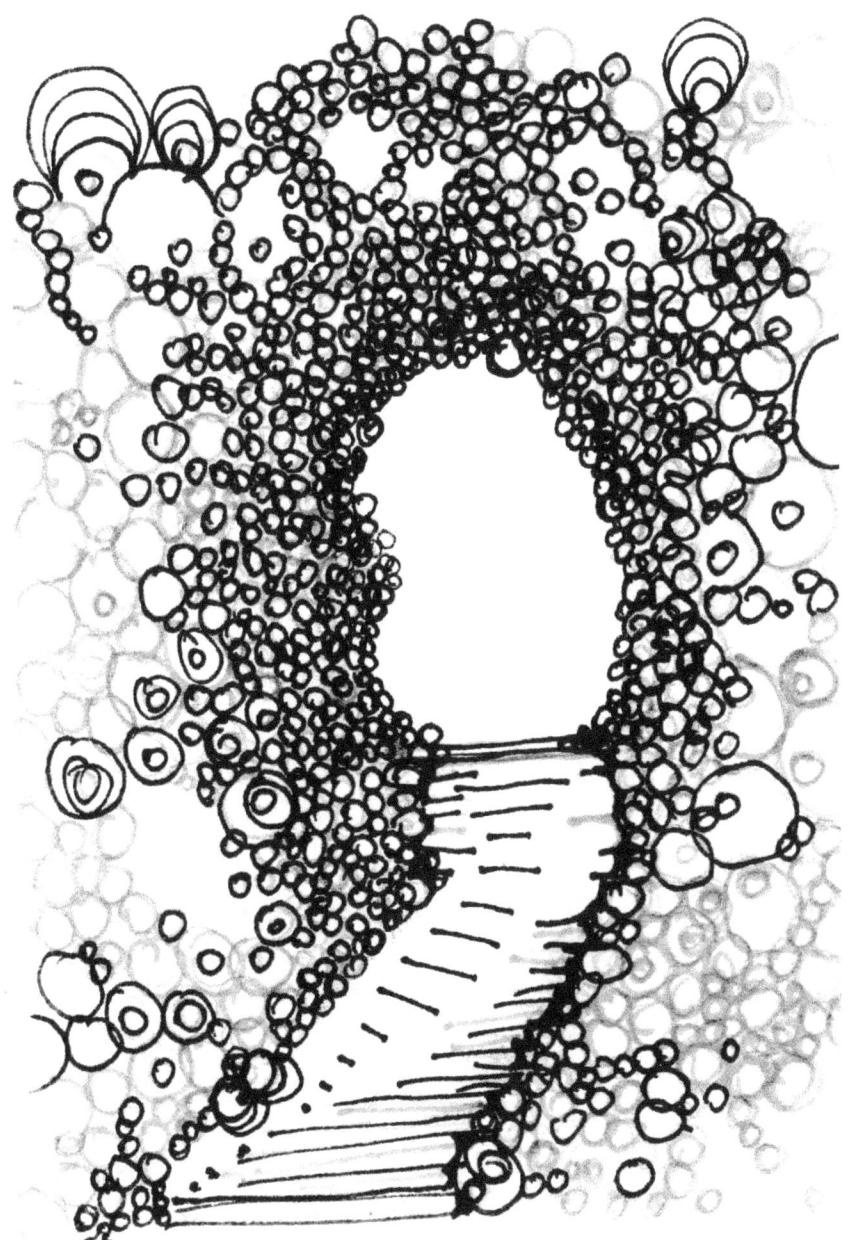

21.

Formless, Untouchable, Intangible.
Elusive yet Real.
Born of the Source.
Formed, Imaged.
Visible with Faith.
Love.
The everlasting offspring of The Source.

22.

In surrender, one finds lasting victory.
Kneeling, one sees The Everlasting Heavens.
To be empty, is to have space for the fullness of life.
In the end there is a new beginning.
To have little is to have space for more.
To have much is to deprive those who have little.
In surrender, kneel.
In emptying, seek to reach the greater awareness of The Source.
Aware of The Source,
One is unobtrusive, yet luminous.
One is humble, yet eminent.
One is empty, yet full.
In line with The Source,
There is immense gratitude for the fullness of life.

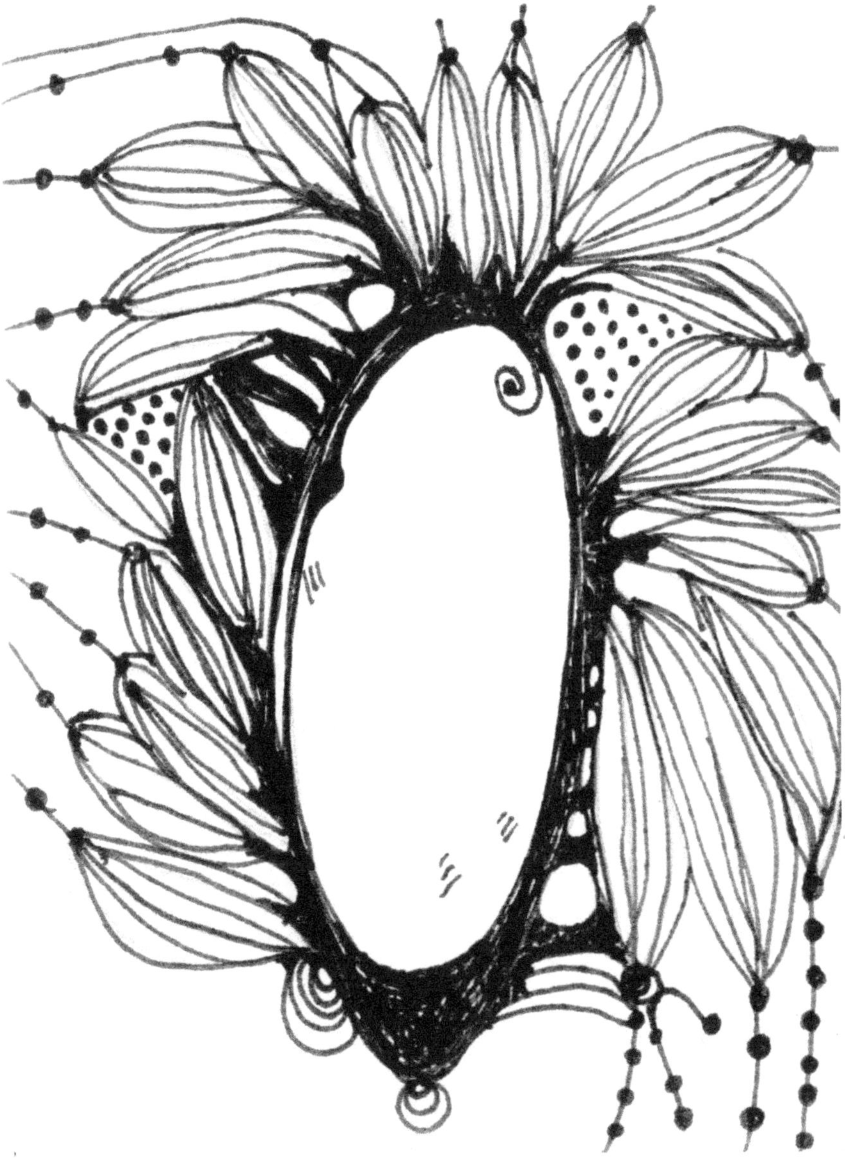

23.

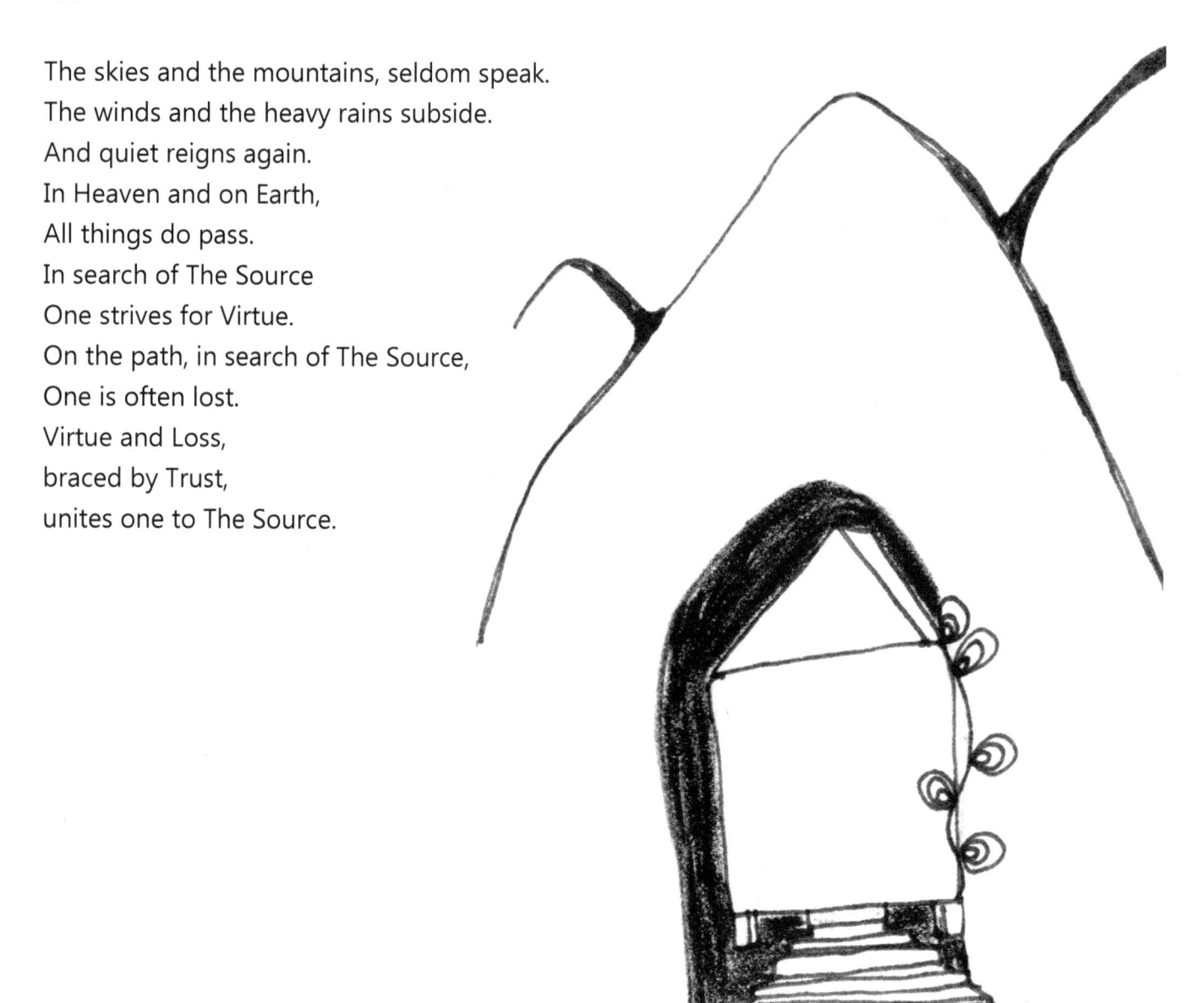

The skies and the mountains, seldom speak.
The winds and the heavy rains subside.
And quiet reigns again.
In Heaven and on Earth,
All things do pass.
In search of The Source
One strives for Virtue.
On the path, in search of The Source,
One is often lost.
Virtue and Loss,
braced by Trust,
unites one to The Source.

24.

With feet planted on the ground,
One is steady.
With measured pace,
One finishes the course,
in comfort.
But
with self-righteousness, boastfulness and braggadocio,
One is assured of the contempt of others.
To follow The Source, the fount of all happiness,
These tendencies must be avoided.

25.
The Beginning is beyond all knowledge.
The Beginning is The Creator.
Unknowable and Unnamed
is The Creator's Beginning.
And yet it is everywhere.
It is everything.
It is The Heavens and The Earth.
Beginning and End.
Unnamed and Unknowable.
The Source.

The root bears the weight of all the branches.
At the bottom of the raging sea there is complete stillness.
On the journey of life,
You must carry all your baggage,
never to be distracted by another man's gold.
The branches sway, yet the roots hold them.
The waters rage, yet the rocks are unmoved.

27.

The path I have walked is littered
with my cracked and crooked footprints.
The words I have spoken are sprinkled
with utterances I should never have thought.
The sums I have tallied
omitted the numbers owed to others,
for their benevolence.
The secrets I have locked away
are all lost to me,
but discoverable by others.
I am,
like my brothers and sisters
Flawed.
It is only The Source
Who walks
without tracks.
Who speaks
Without errors.
Who reckons
with precision.
Who unlocks
All secrets.
It is The Source
who cares for all.
Regardless of our frailties.

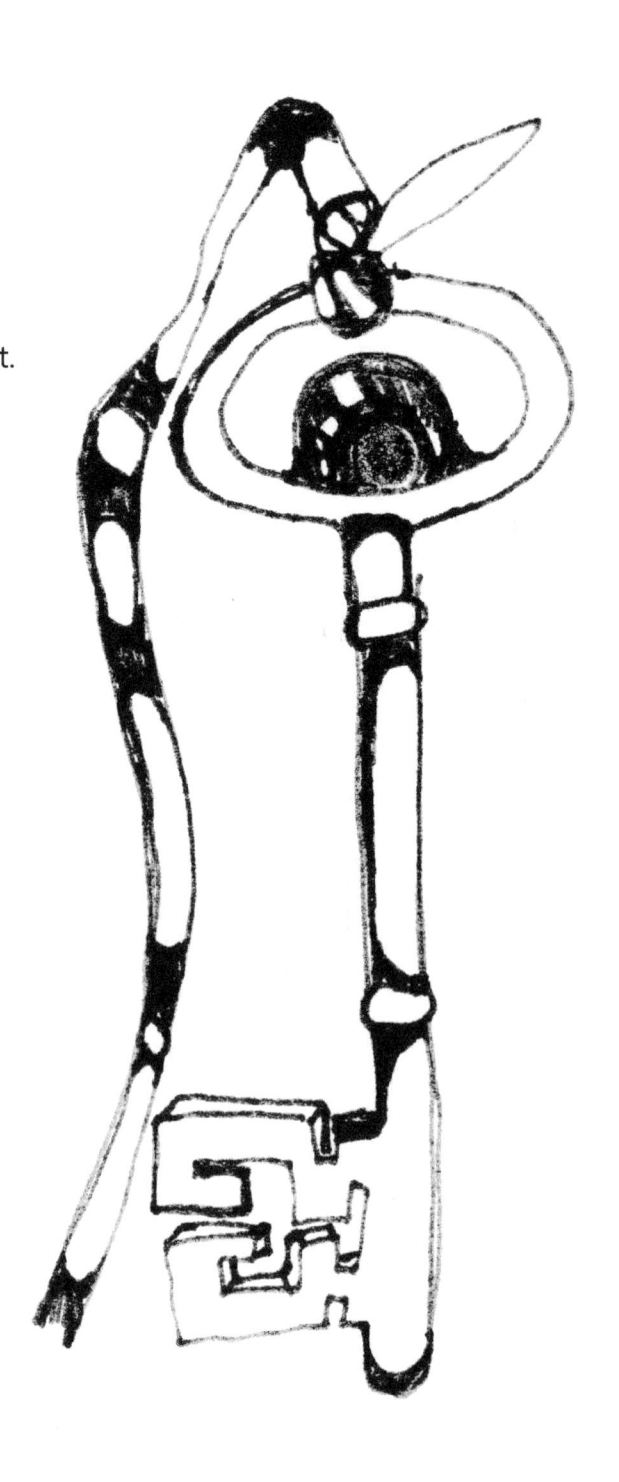

Strength without caring
is power to abuse.
Caring with strength
is the balance of forces.
The balance of forces is the essence of Nature.

Coloured and colourless.
Black and white.
Rivers and Veins.
Travelling to eternity.

Honour without humility
is but arrogance.
Prominence with humility
begets a tempered disposition.
The balance of forces is the essence of Nature.
Open, unfixed in thought
is to be at one with Nature.
At one with Nature,
One is in tune with Eternity.

29.

The Universe is not mine to alter.
To possess the universe is the desire of the ego
though it is beyond the capacity of mere transients.
The Universe unfolds.
Sometimes at pace,
sometimes slowly.
Sometimes to one's benefit,
sometimes to one's detriment.
Sometimes with great joy,
sometimes with unbearable sorrow.
Unalterable
The Universe unfolds.
The challenge for our journey,
is to travel like The Sage,
without desire,
in the flow of The Universe.

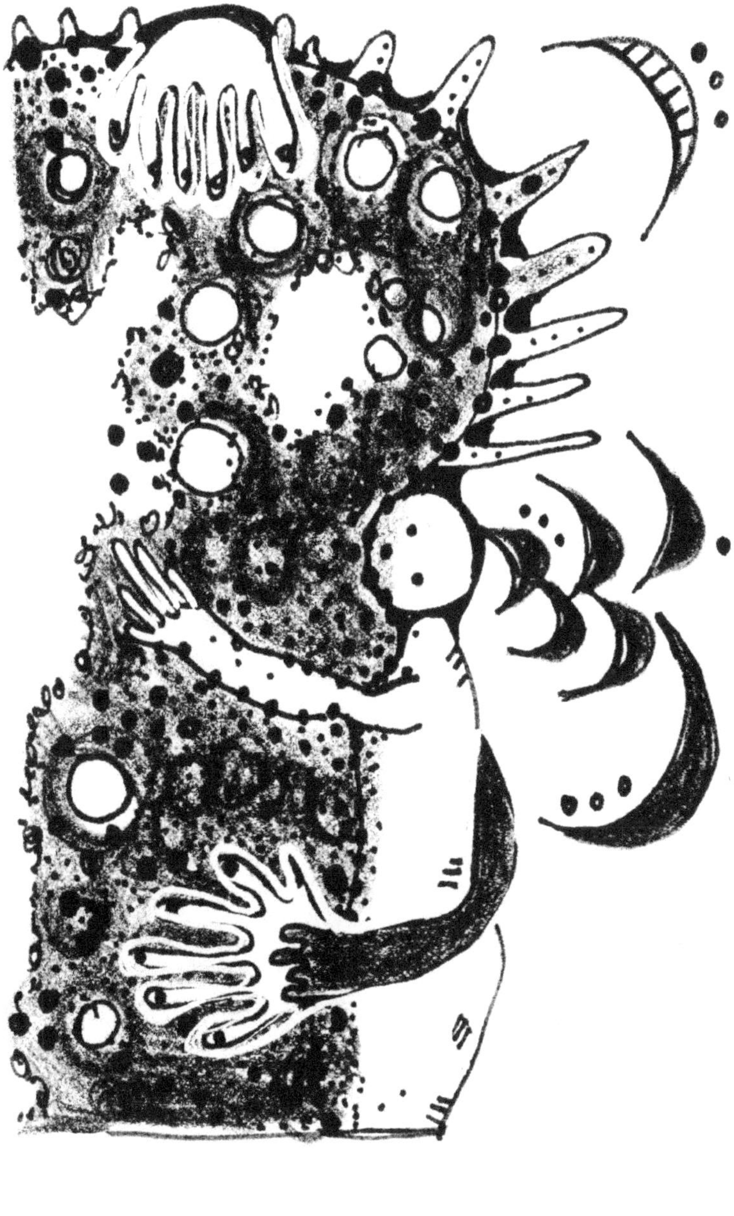

30.

To achieve lasting results, refrain from using force.
A quiet word engenders much less resistance than force.
Alignment with The Source leads to acceptance of all that is.
Be humble in achievement.
Be quiet in fulfillment.
Be nonviolent in all actions.
To be strong is to be vulnerable.
To be vulnerable is to submit to the all-encompassing Source.
To submit to The Source is to know no ending.

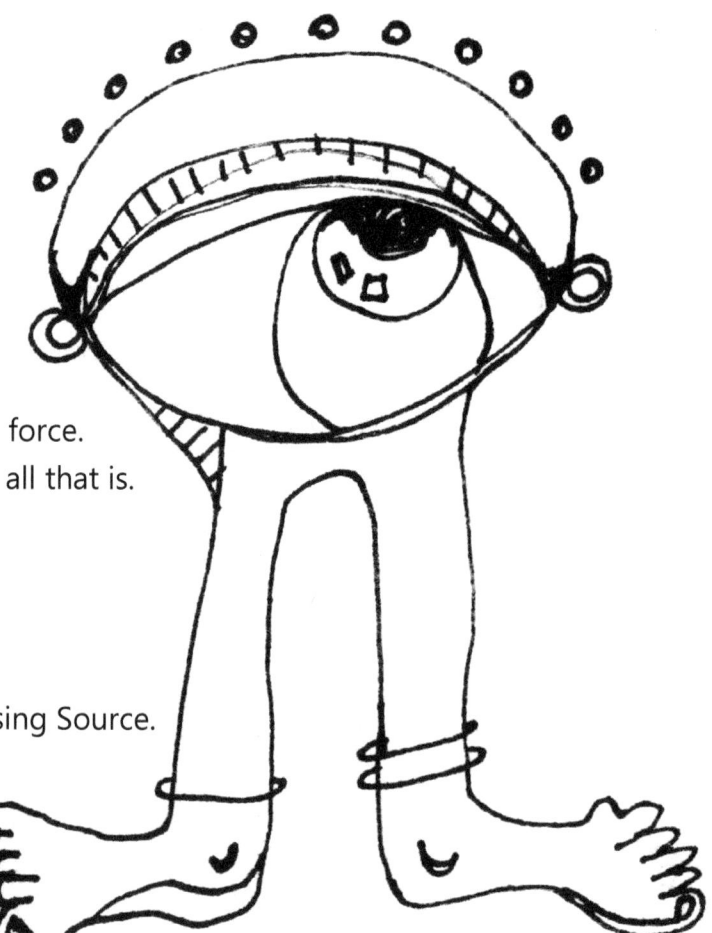

31.

Weapons, instruments of violence, create fear.
Where there is fear, calm is never present.
Where calm is absent, love cannot flourish.
Wisdom encourages the calming of the mind.
With a clam mind, there is little need for weaponry.
Peace and quiet prevail in both winning and losing.
Neither victory or defeat are of any consequence.
    Without peace and quiet there is much room for violence.
    Where there is room for violence, there is much fear.
    In victory, won through violence and fear,
    The victors will eventually be the losers.
    And the Vanquished will rise in the embrace
      wof The Source.

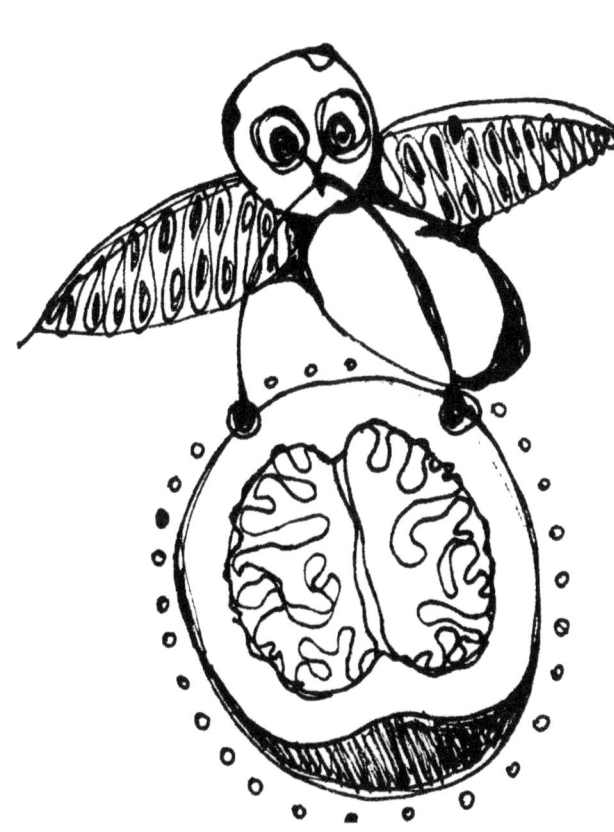

32.

Before Now and in Time to come,
The Source remains undefined.
It is Unknowable, Invisible, Intangible.
And yet we yearn to learn, to see to touch.
We profess to know The Heavens.
We profess to know The Earth,
From whence we came,
to where we will return
neither knowing the time or place of our demise.
We are never satisfied with our imperfect knowledge.
Comfort arrives only when we willingly surrender to The Source
to be carried along by its Unknowable, Invisible, Intangible force.
In its embrace, we meld into the essence of everything,
We are one with the Unknowable, Invisible, Intangible Source.

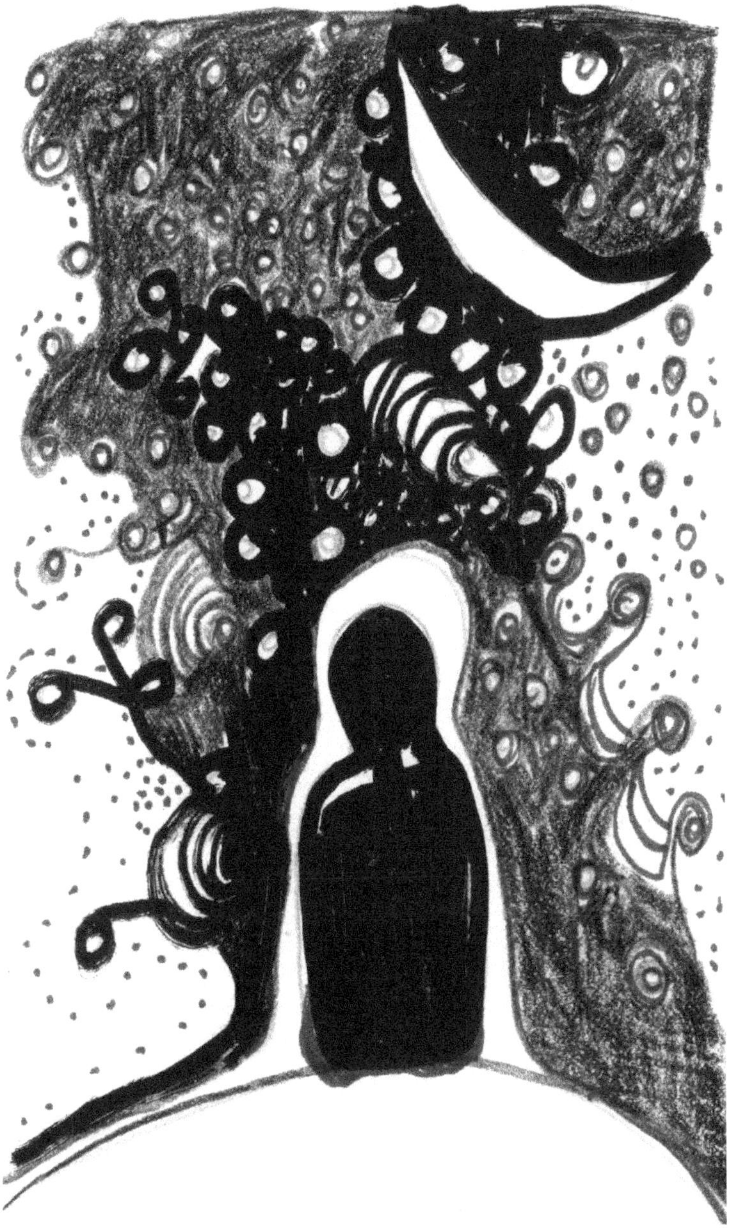

33.

Through observation, knowledge is accumulated.
Through the accumulation of knowledge, wisdom is gained.
Through introspection, self-knowledge is accumulated.
Through the accumulation of self-knowledge, strength is gained.
With strength and wisdom, one is satisfied with one's lot.
He who is satisfied makes provision for the satisfaction of others.
He who makes provision for the satisfaction of others
seamlessly blends into the Eternal Giver, The Source.

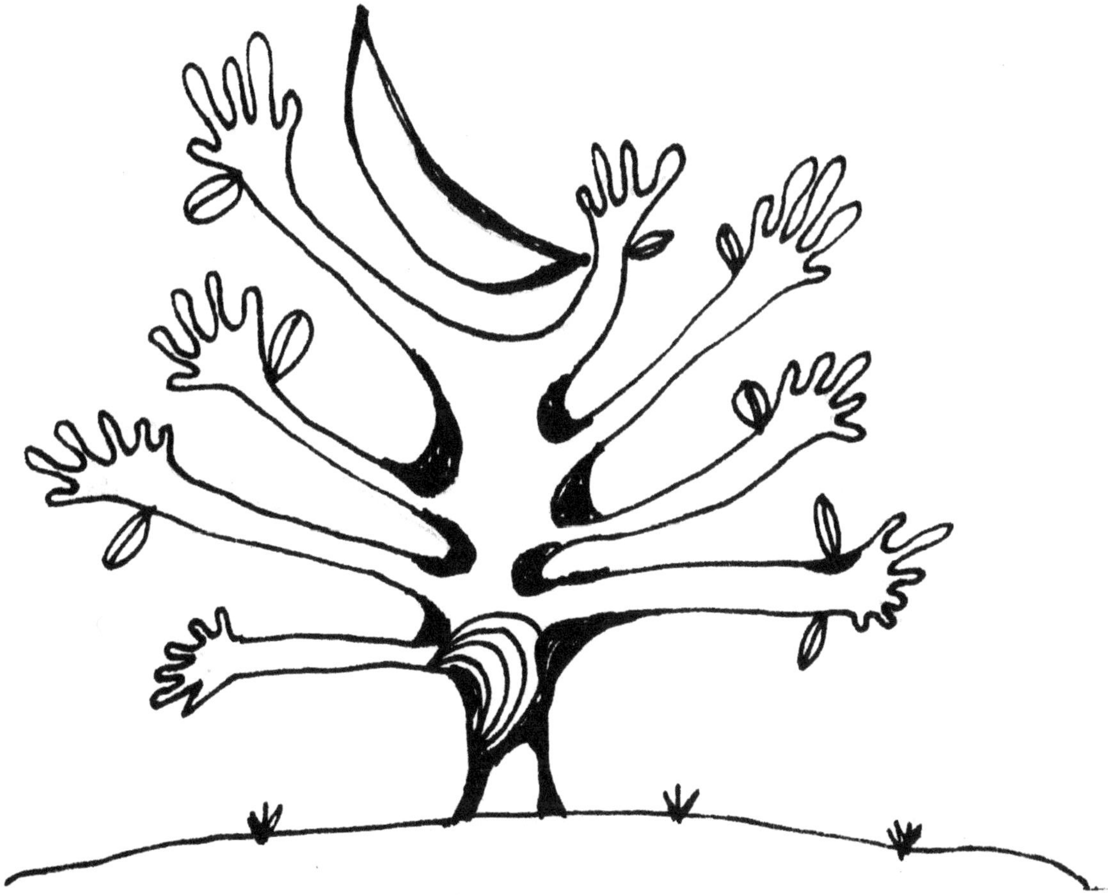

34.

Virtue is ever present.

Above

                                        Below.

Visible

                                        Invisible

Virtue embraces all things.

The Good.

                                        The bad.

The Poor

                                        The great.

The Small

                                        The big.

All things must embrace Virtue.
Virtue is always visible where there is humility.
Only that which is humble is truly Great.

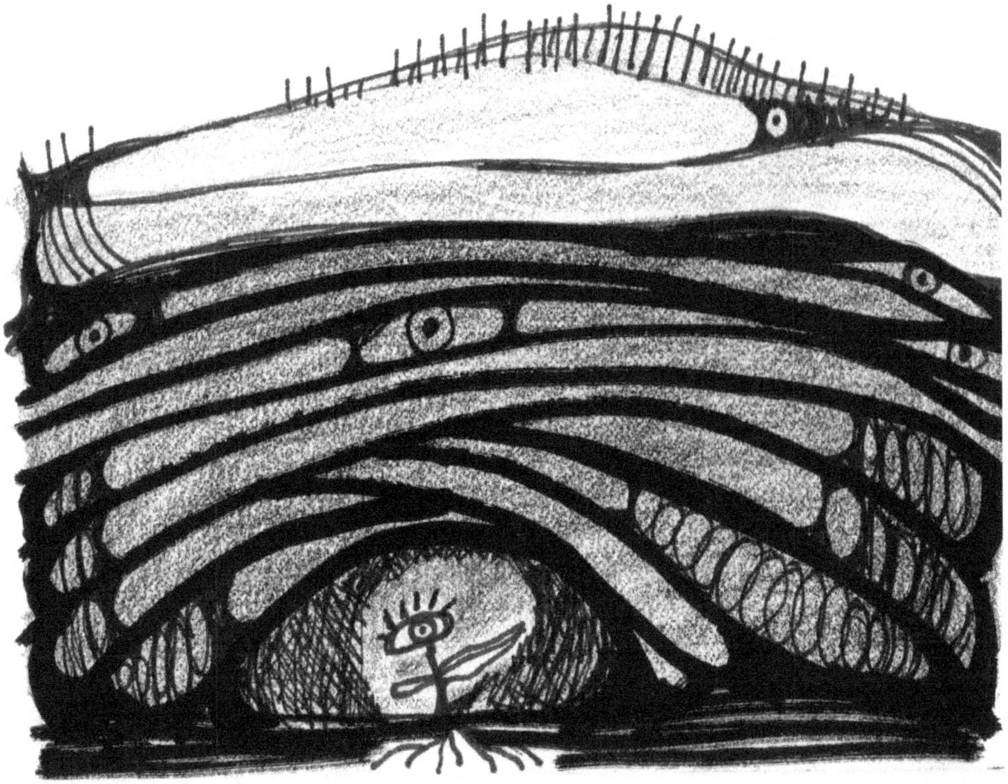

35.

In search of happiness and lasting peace,
We seek The Source.
Along the way,
song and dance,
wine and good fare,
Family and Friends
help guide the Way.
Yet, never ever quite getting there,
We keep seeking.
Always knowing that
The Infinite Love of
The Unknowable
is beyond our reach,
beyond our comprehension.
And seek we must.

Growth precedes shrinkage.
Nothing stays the same.
Strength precedes weakness.
All things must change.
Elevation precedes decline,
Nothing stays the same.
Giving precedes receiving.
All things must change.
Still, the fish belong to the waters.
The weapons should never leave the armoury,
For Nothing,
Stays the same.

37.

Being quiet, one hears the World.
Being still, one feels the Heavens.
Being blind, one sees the Universe.
The World, The Heavens, The Universe,
All forms of The Formless Source.
Eternal Peace exists.
In the blindingly still quietude of The Formless Source.

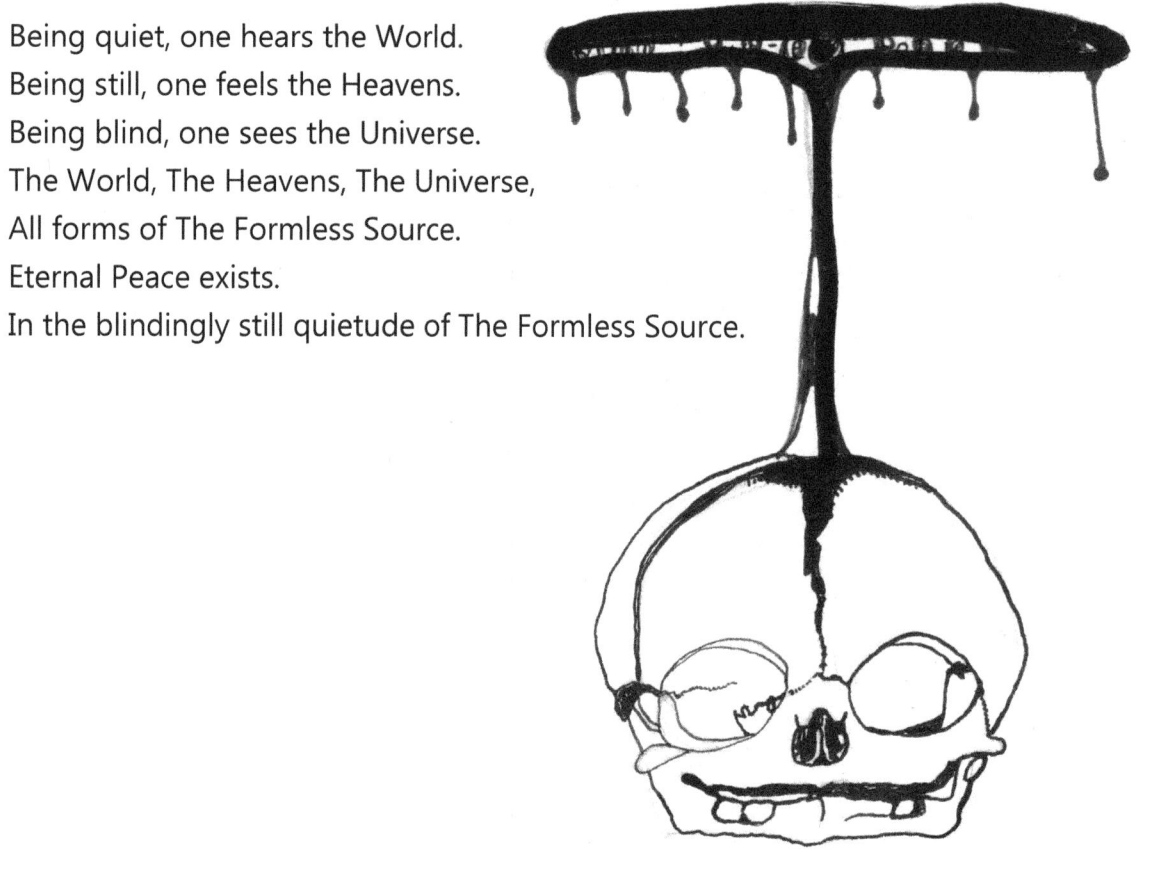

38.

I look into the mirror,
to measure my goodness.
I see my flaws.
A good man looks at the world,
to see its beauty.
The world sees his goodness.
The beauty of the world
does nothing to itself
to be revealed.
It is resplendent in its inaction.
I am constantly doing.
For my betterment.
The world hardly notices.
Was I kind?
Am I kind?
Will I be kind in the future?
Was I good?
Am I good?
Will I be good in the future?
Was I just?
Am I just?
Will I be just in the future?
Was I wise?
Am I wise?
Will I be wise in the future?
Who will be the judge of all these questions?
Surely not me.
Like The Heavens, The Earth, and its Everlasting Source,
I would do well to favour inaction.

39.

From one eternal source, all spring.
The Heavens,
The Earth,
The Soul,
All are alive in the wellspring of The Source.
Each part of an indivisible whole.
The Whole is Perpetual.
Forever, The Heavens hover above The Earth.
Forever, The Earth embraces all living things.
Forever, The Soul transits The Heavens and The Earth,
For a little while kings reign on Earth.
With humility good kings embrace all living things.
Good Kings are guardians of The Earth.
Their success is not the crown that adorns their heads,
But the peace that engulfs living things.

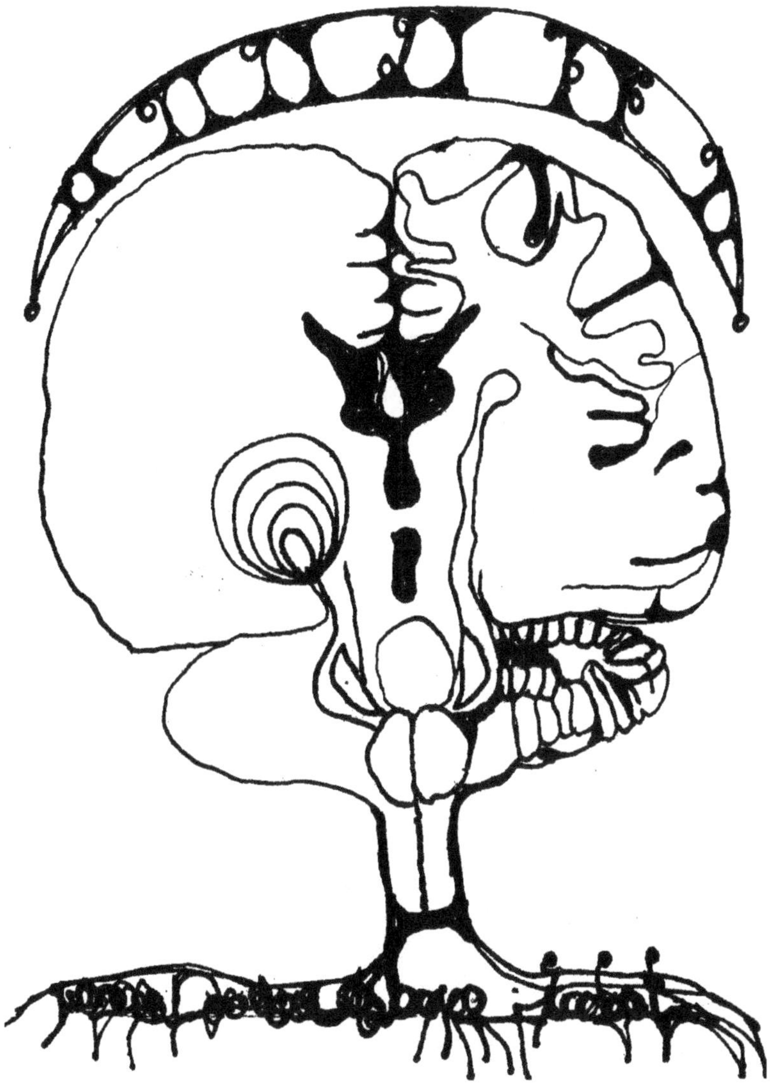

40.

From whence all came,
All return.
From The Source,
all take.
To The Source,
All must be given.
Beginning and Ending.
Both fuse into the Everlasting Unknown
that is The Source.

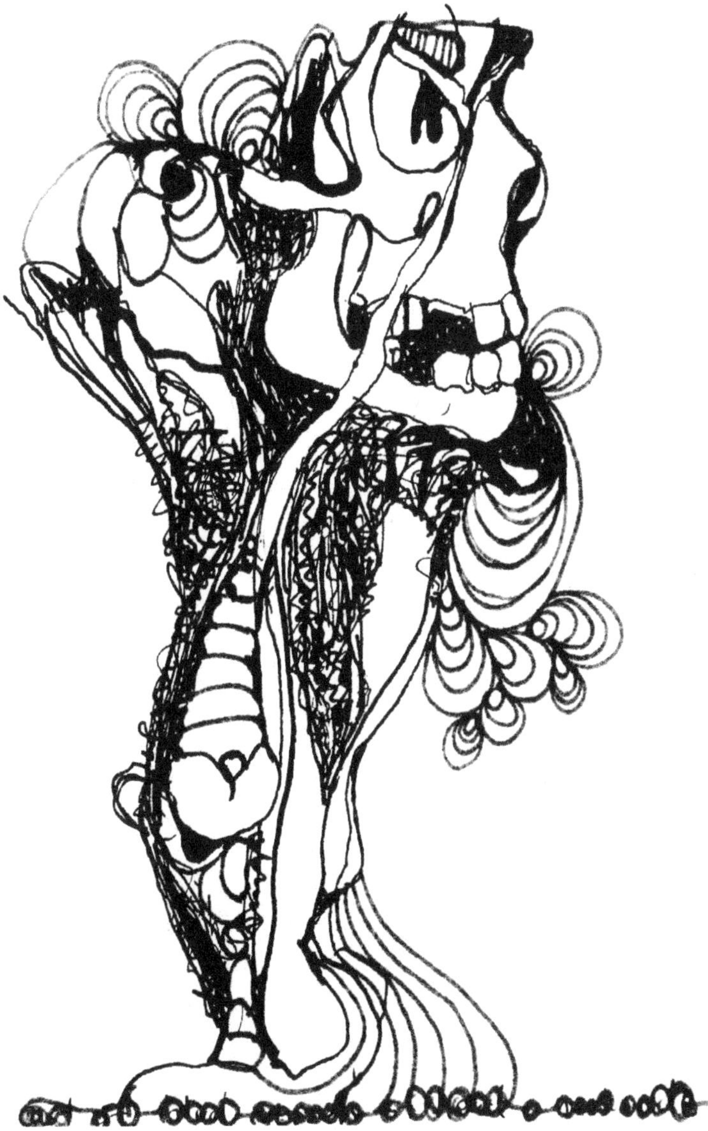

41.

All hear the eternal truth,
A few pursue it diligently.
Many recognize it casually in passing,
As they fervently pursue the temporal.
A few dismiss it passionately.
The Truth embraces them all, for eternity.
To some, the light is darkness.
To some, retreat is progress.
To some, pain is relief.
Virtue and Purity
are despised by a few.
For some, weakness is strength.
For some, richness is poverty.
For some, words are weapons.
Virtue and Purity
inspire many.
Shapeless and wordless,
From The Source, Eternal,
springs,
Virtue and Purity.

In the beginning there was One.
The One was The Whole.
The Whole was not sufficient unto itself.
And so, there were many.
After the beginning,
The Whole and its parts,
Joy and Pain,
Gain and Loss,
Life and Death,
All became One with The Whole.
As it was in The Beginning.

43.

No stone is so hard that it cannot be shaped by Water.
No heart is so closed that it cannot be opened by Love.
Both water and love,
emanating from The Eternal Source,
Shower blessings on all.

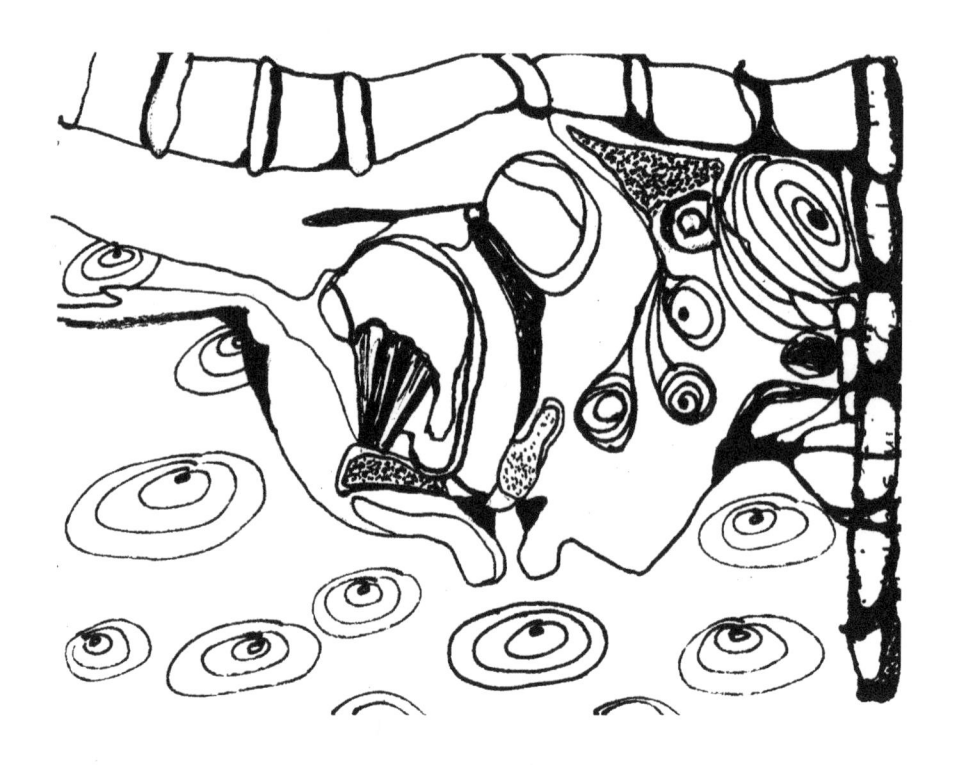

Along the way to fame
the self may be lost.
Along the way to riches,
the self may be sold.
Lost and sold,
the self is selfish.
Humble and poor,
the self is selfless.
A selfish self is never at ease.
A selfless self is ever contented.
Ever contented,
The Self is in tune with
The Virtues of Life.

45.

Meaningful accomplishment
is always modestly declared.
Its true measure is its enduring usefulness.
Estimation of enough
js always where there is room for more.
Its true measure is what is available to share.
Sometimes, the straight path may seem to have deviations.
Sometimes, the wise may seem foolish.
Sometimes, the eloquent may sound choked.
The cold is warmed by movement.
The heart is cooled by stillness.
Movement and Heat,
Stillness and Cold,
They order the Universe.

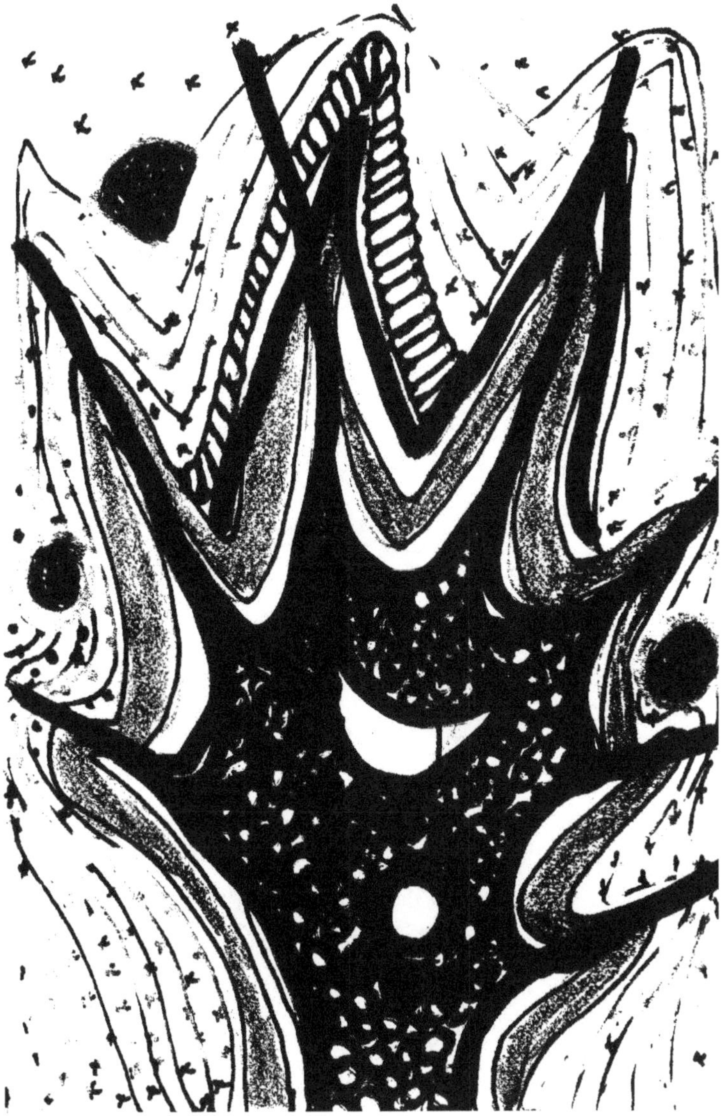

46.

Where Virtue and Love prevail,
Men attend to the wellbeing of all creatures.
Where envy and hate prevail,
Men attend to the destruction of all creatures.
hate and envy beget discontent.
Discontent is the portal to selfishness.
Selfishness is the portal to greed.
Where Virtue and Love prevail,
It is possible to discern what is enough.

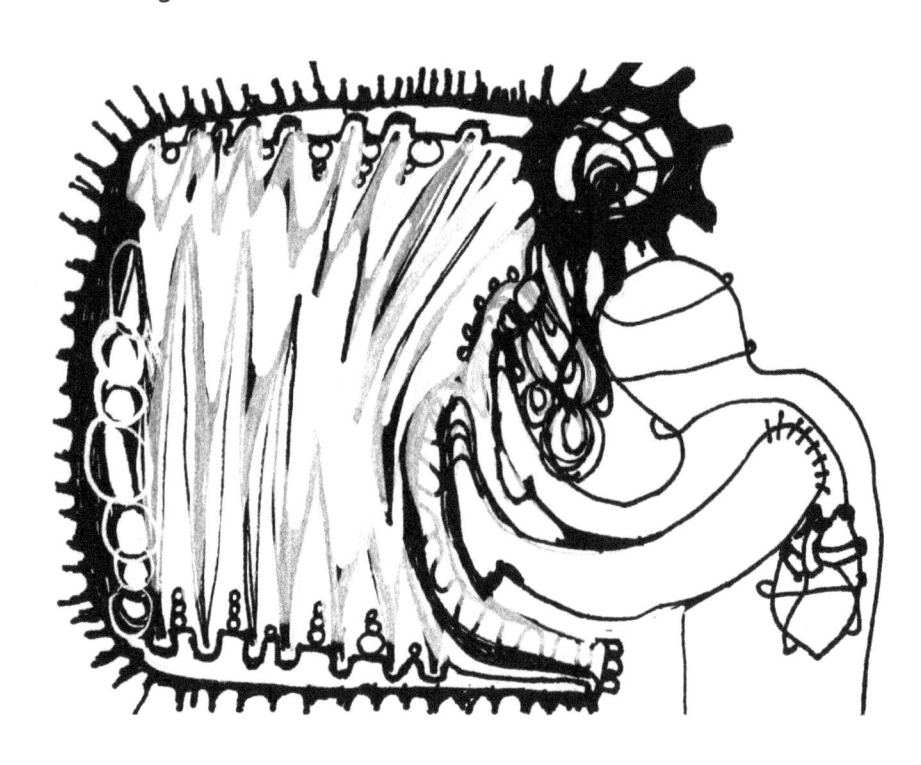

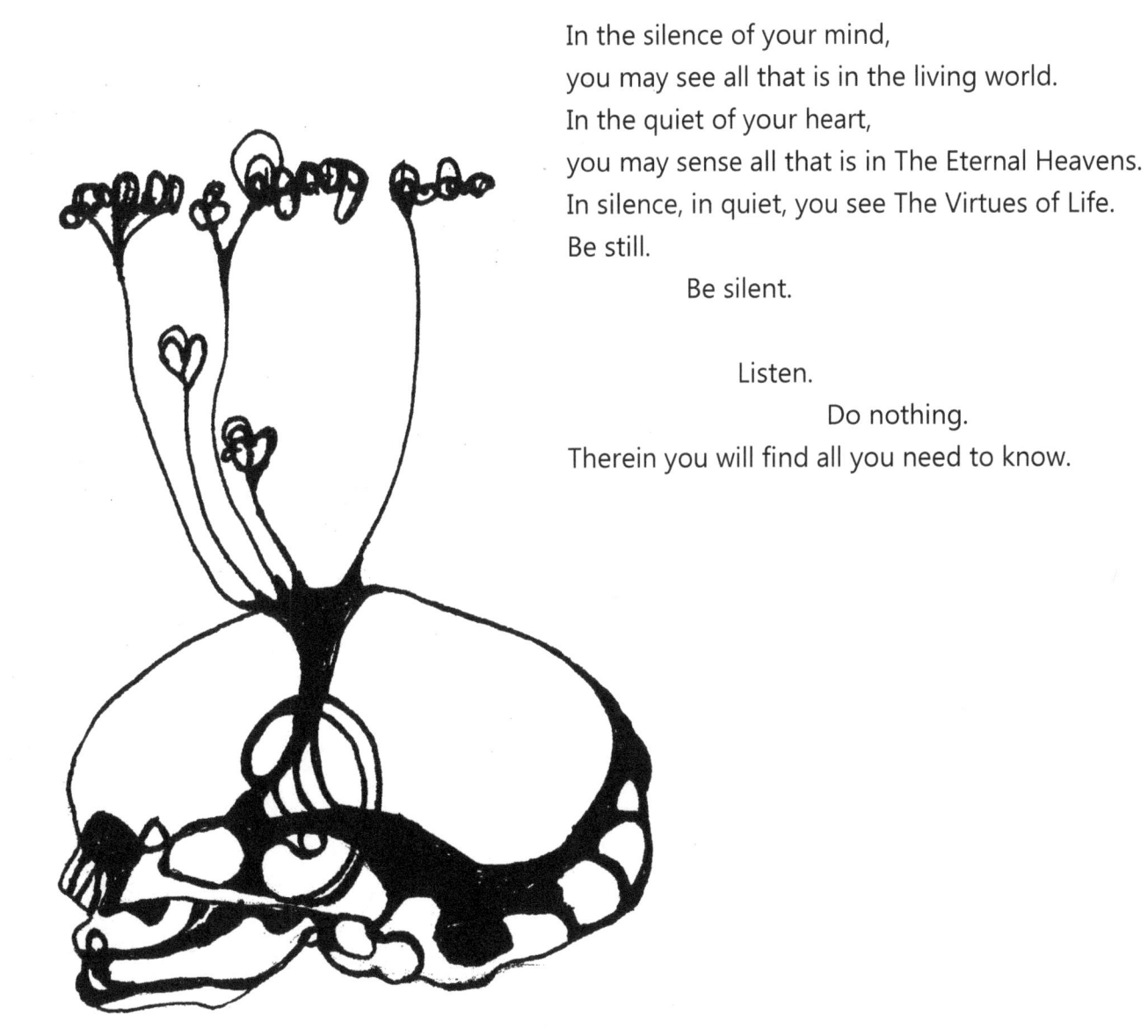

In the silence of your mind,
you may see all that is in the living world.
In the quiet of your heart,
you may sense all that is in The Eternal Heavens.
In silence, in quiet, you see The Virtues of Life.
Be still.
        Be silent.

       Listen.
             Do nothing.
Therein you will find all you need to know.

48.

In pursuit of a good life,
each day is an act of accumulation,
of days, of knowledge and wealth.
In pursuit of Eternity,
Each day is an act of decumulation,
of days, of ego and material possessions.
Less is left,
and less and less is left to be done.
In the end,
there is nothing to be done,
except to accept that The Source
always requires
Nothing to be done.

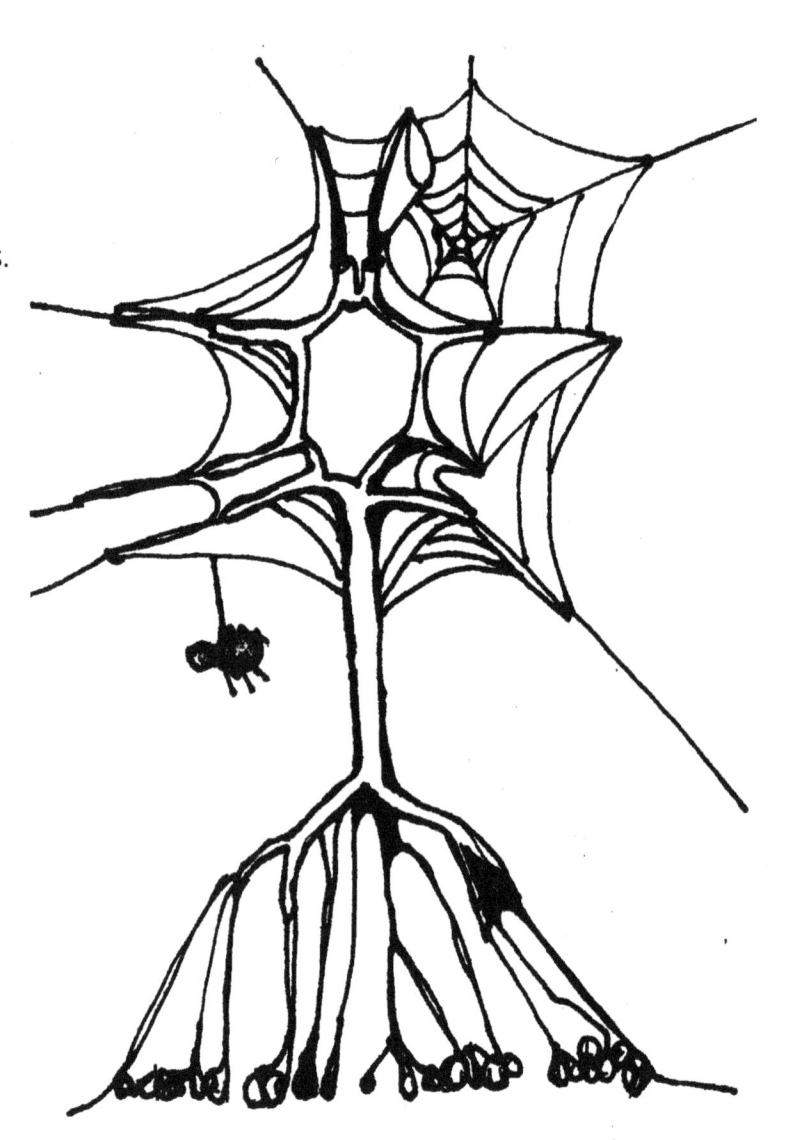

Singularity of purpose and mind blinds one to the needs of others.
Seeing the needs of others blinds one to their shortcomings.
To see the other, is the way of Virtue.
Goodness and Faithfulness abound in the eye of Virtue.
It is Virtue that aligns the living with The Eternal Source.

50.

In living, few manage the challenges of Life.
In living, few manage the challenge of Death.
Many manage only to pass from living to dying.
He who manages the fear of living,
He who manages the peace of dying,
Lives and dies without transition.
He is the servant of his eternal soul.

The Nothingness of 5The Source is the Fount of Virtue.
From the Nothingness of The Source, all things come forth
As matter.
All matter is The Source.
All matter is the vessel of Virtue.
Nothingness in matter.
Virtue, from Nothingness.
Nothingness, Virtue, Matter.
All from the everlasting Fount,
The Source.

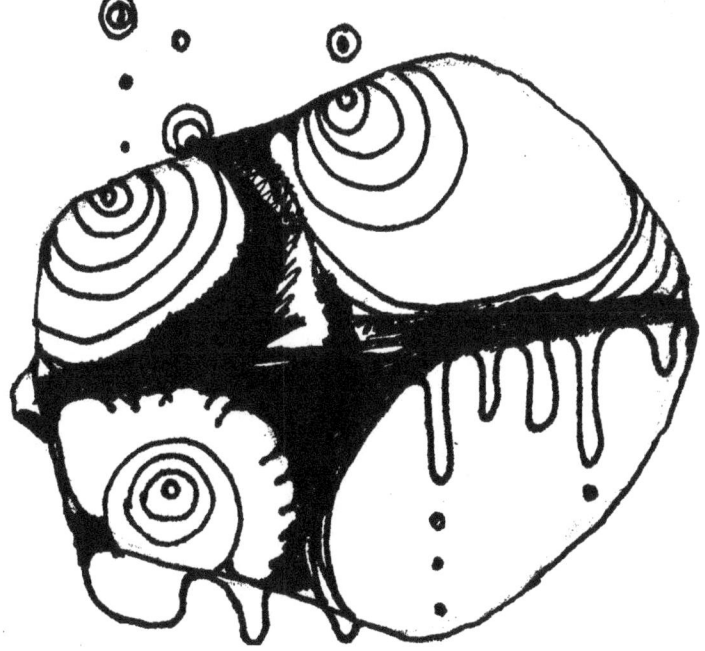

52.

Everything begins with Virtue.
Virtue is the manifest quality of The Universe.
Virtue is the maternal force of all Matter.
With knowledge of Matter,
The born are in tune with Virtue.
The Mother, the giver of knowledge to the born,
is the unbreakable link between birth and death.
In silence, the senses are best protected.
There, Virtue embodies Life.
Noisily, the senses are exposed.
There, hope in life expires.
Sight of the small brings insight.
Acceptance of force yields strength.
Humility reflects the inner light
that is the connection of matter to knowledge.
Little harm can come from the constancy of silence and peace.

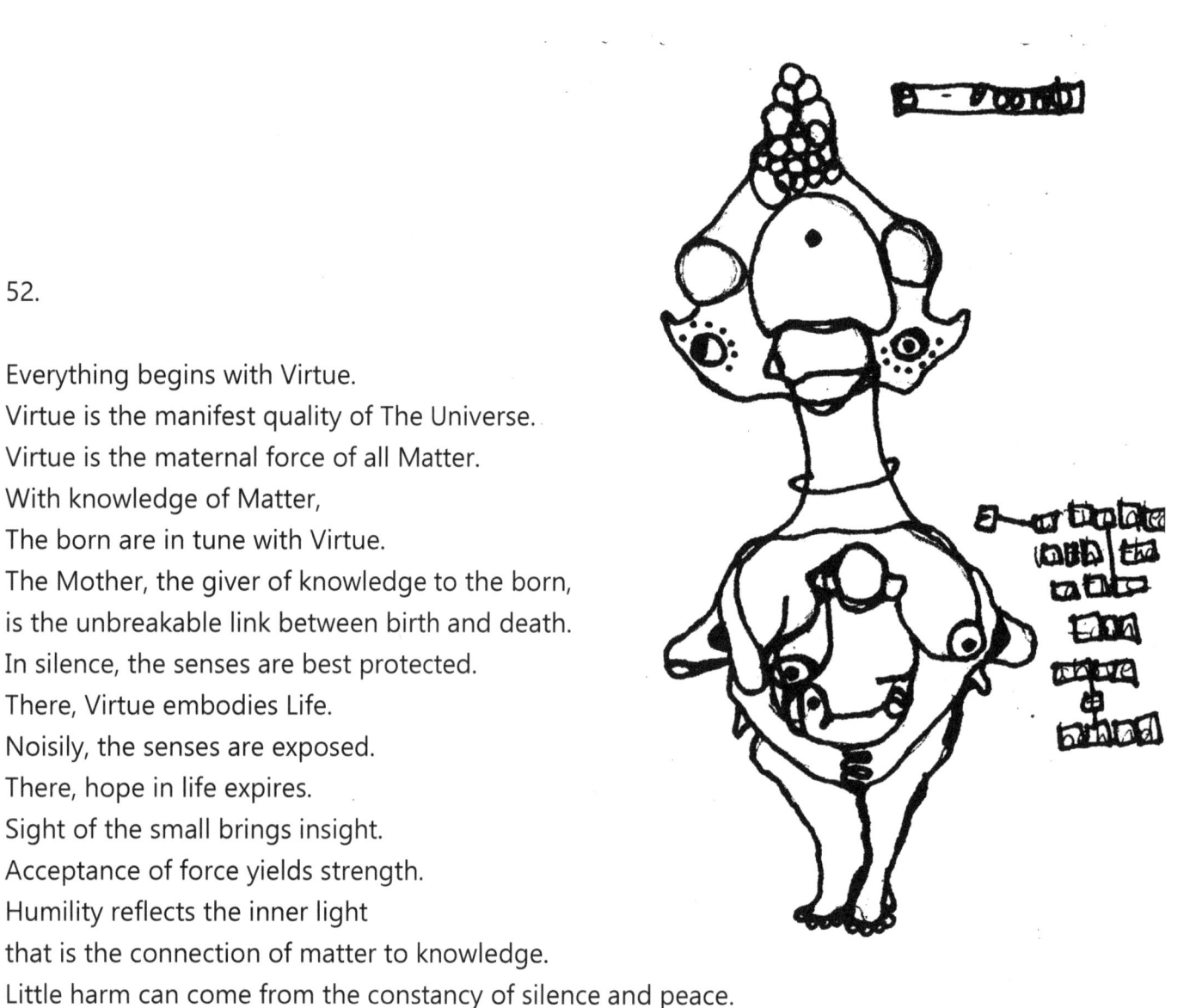

A virtuous path is the path worth following on a life worth living.
And yet it is so easy to diverge.
Attractions abound on the least virtuous paths.
And so, we build monuments of opulence
And ignore the surrounding squalor.
We shower our bodies with resplendence.
 And ignore the naked.
  We devour and imbibe with indulgence.
   And ignore the hungry.
    Ever striving for more than
     Enough.
      The paths divergent that we so readily choose
       Are forever at odds with the Virtue that is The Source.

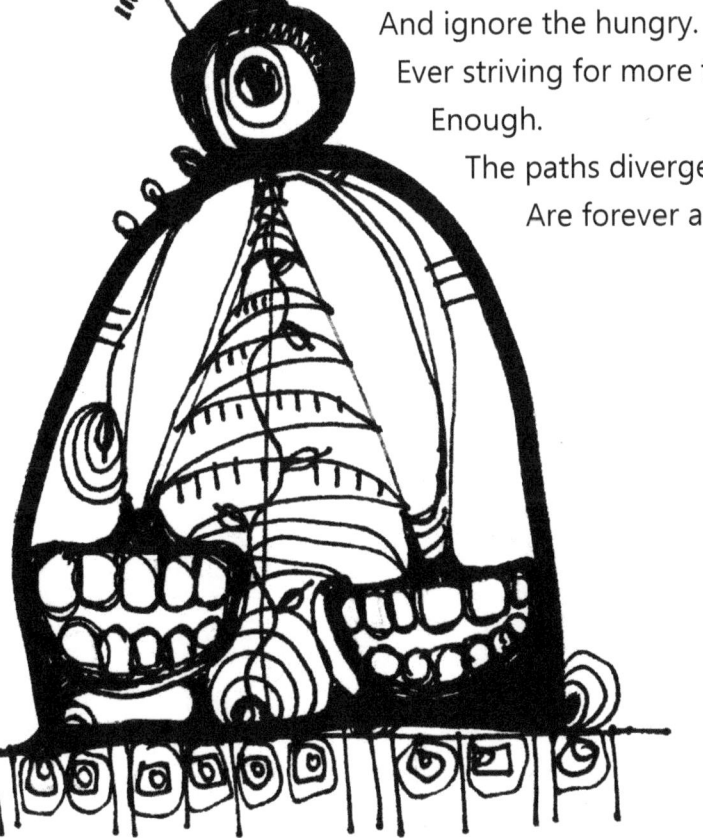

54.

That which is fully grounded cannot be extirpated.
That which is fully comprehended cannot dissipate.
That which is grounded and comprehended will flow through generations.
To be grounded in self, Virtue is required.
To be grounded in family, Virtue is aplenty.
To be grounded in the village, Virtue is ever increasing.
To be grounded in the nation, Virtue is in abundance.
Where Virtue is cultivated in self, in family, in village in nation,
The Universe is at peace.
Look therefore at the self, the family, the village , the nation
All grounded in Virtue,
There one sees the Universe, in its true state,
A state of virtuous peace.

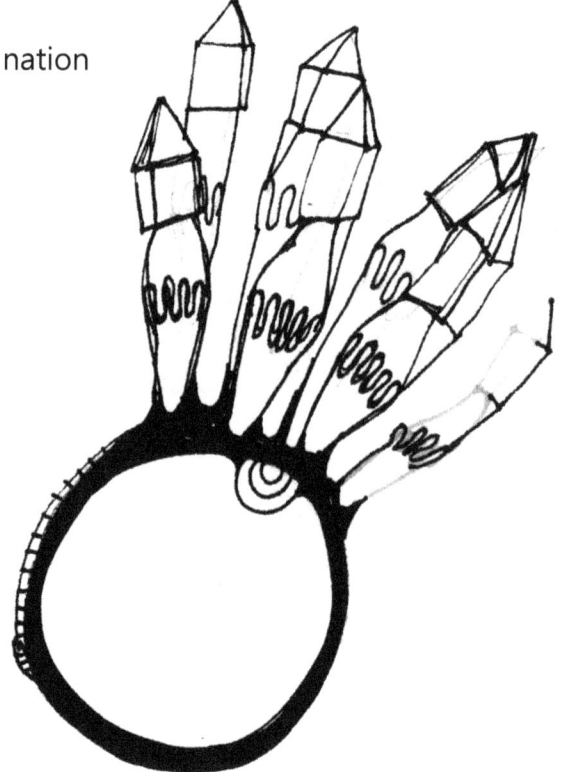

55.

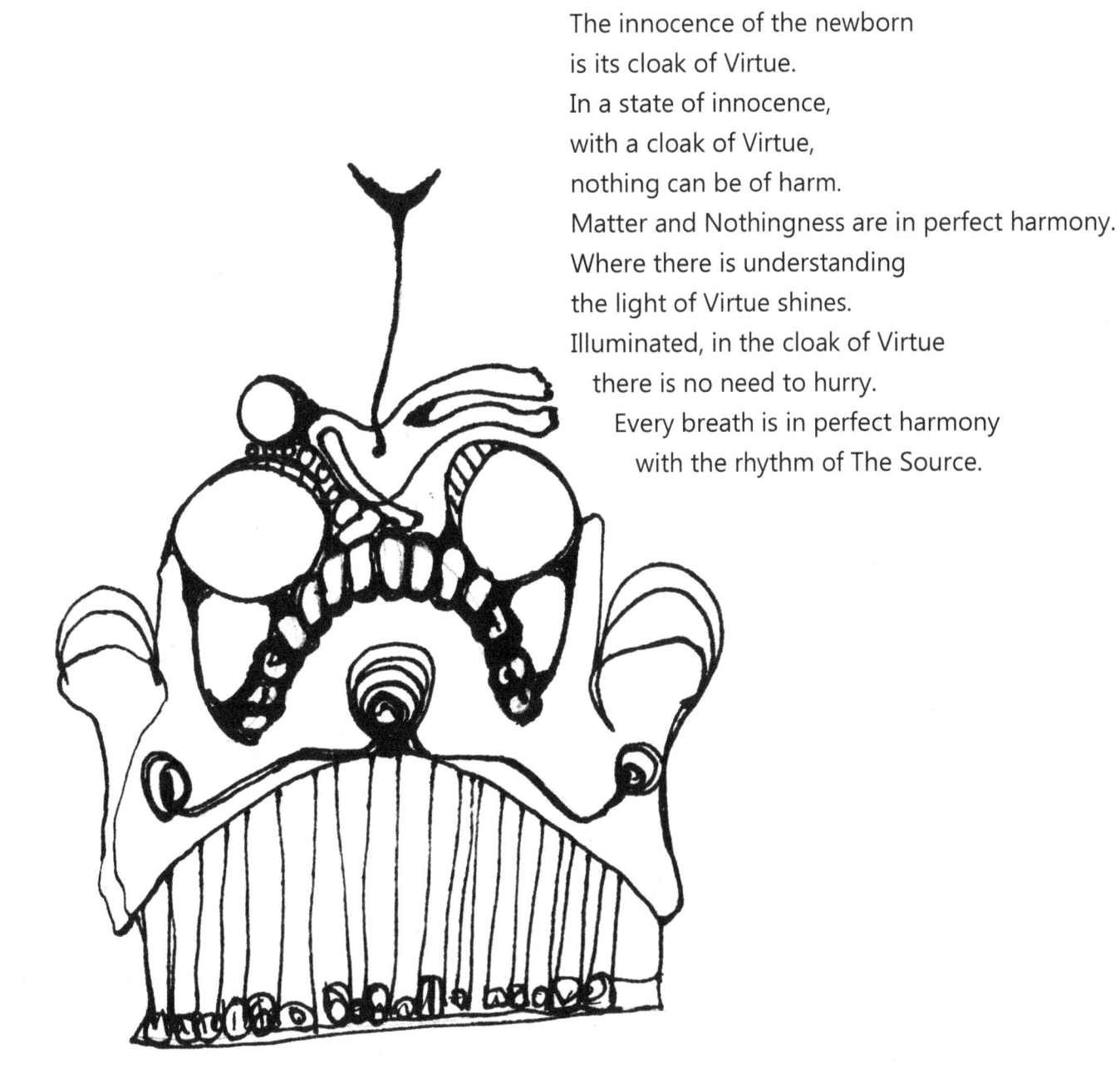

The innocence of the newborn
is its cloak of Virtue.
In a state of innocence,
with a cloak of Virtue,
nothing can be of harm.
Matter and Nothingness are in perfect harmony.
Where there is understanding
the light of Virtue shines.
Illuminated, in the cloak of Virtue
  there is no need to hurry.
    Every breath is in perfect harmony
      with the rhythm of The Source.

56.

He who knows, utters not a word.
The uttered words come
from he who knows not.
In silence, with grounded senses,
He who knows, is ever humble.
He is in tune with the Earth.
Ever mindful that
it is the dust from whence he came.
He embraces all around him.
He readies himself for his
inevitable return
to the Earth,
his Source.

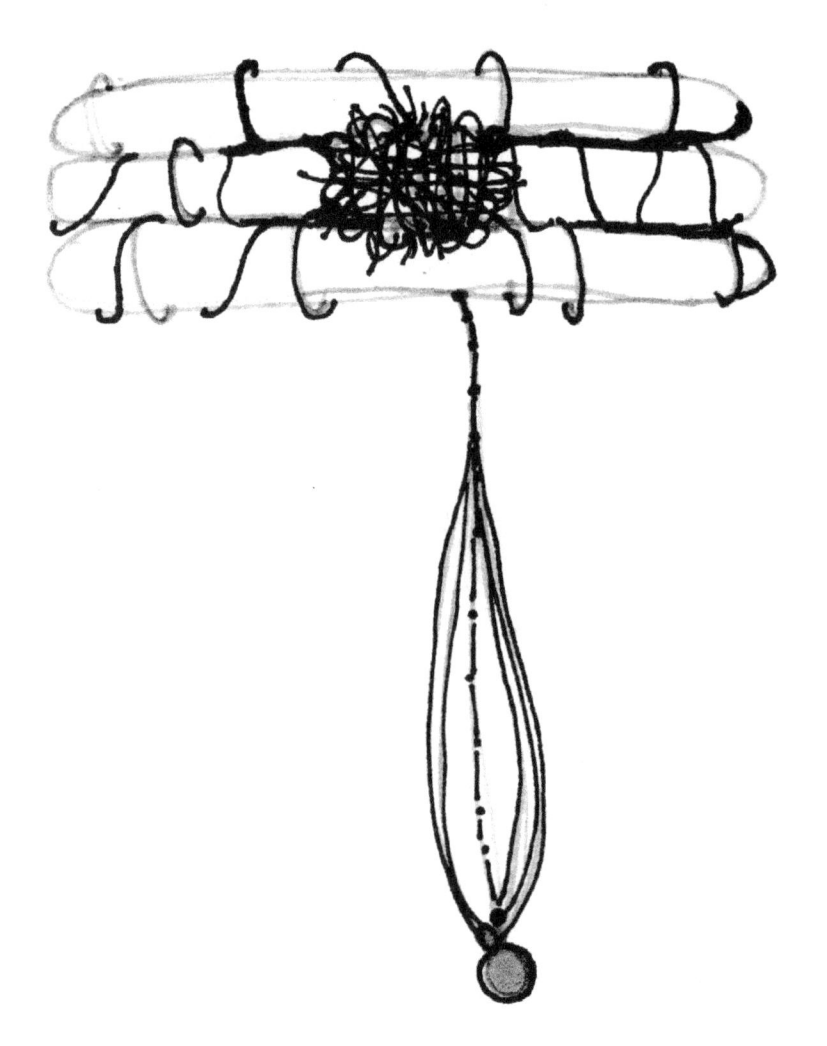

A good leader is just and fair.
He does not foment conflict.
He is slow to anger and even slower to wage war.
Like the Sage,
his infrequent wars are utter surprises.
A good leader is peaceful.
A good leader is kind.
A good leader leads a simple life.
The people seek to emulate a good leader,

The people are honest and morally enriched,
The people are content.
In concert, a good leader and an honest people
embrace the simplicity that is the hallmark of the Sage.

58.

A people led with fairness and equanimity
are well tempered and simple,
A people led with bias and harshness
are ill tempered and conniving.
Connivance is the kinfolk of conflict.
Misery and Happiness too, are kinfolk.
They dwell together in all people,
Never telling each other,
when the other might alight.
They arrive one after the other,
Again, and again.
Happiness
Then Misery,
Misery,
Then Happiness.
The people are confused.
Is happiness real?
Is misery an illusion?
Is there Truth?
What is untrue?
These are the questions,
For all ages.
The Sage is silent.
Quiet and Simple .
He knows that all are
part of the Insoluble Whole.

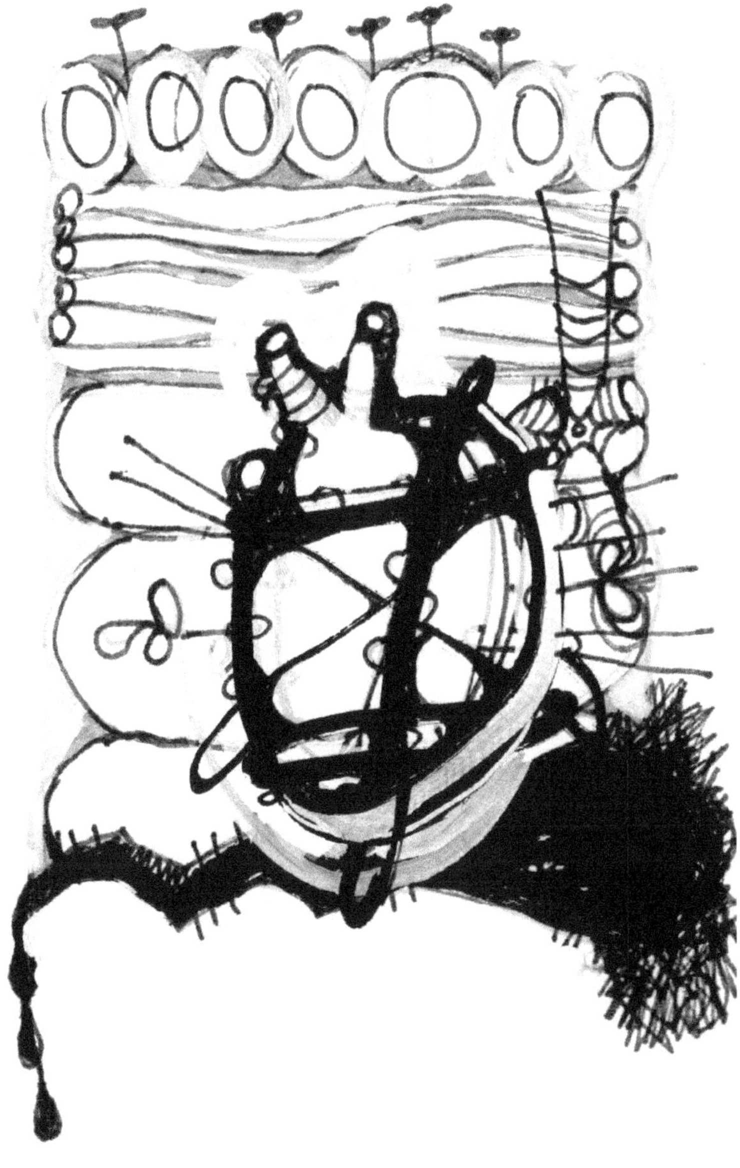

59.

To serve Heaven is simple.
All that is required
is that we care for others
without the constraint of self.
Where Virtue is accumulated
serving Heaven is simplicity.
Where simplicity is present,
It is possible to lead virtuously.

To lead virtuously is to serve others without restraint.
To lead with simplicity is to be in tune
with The Everlasting Source,
The Mother of all Creation.

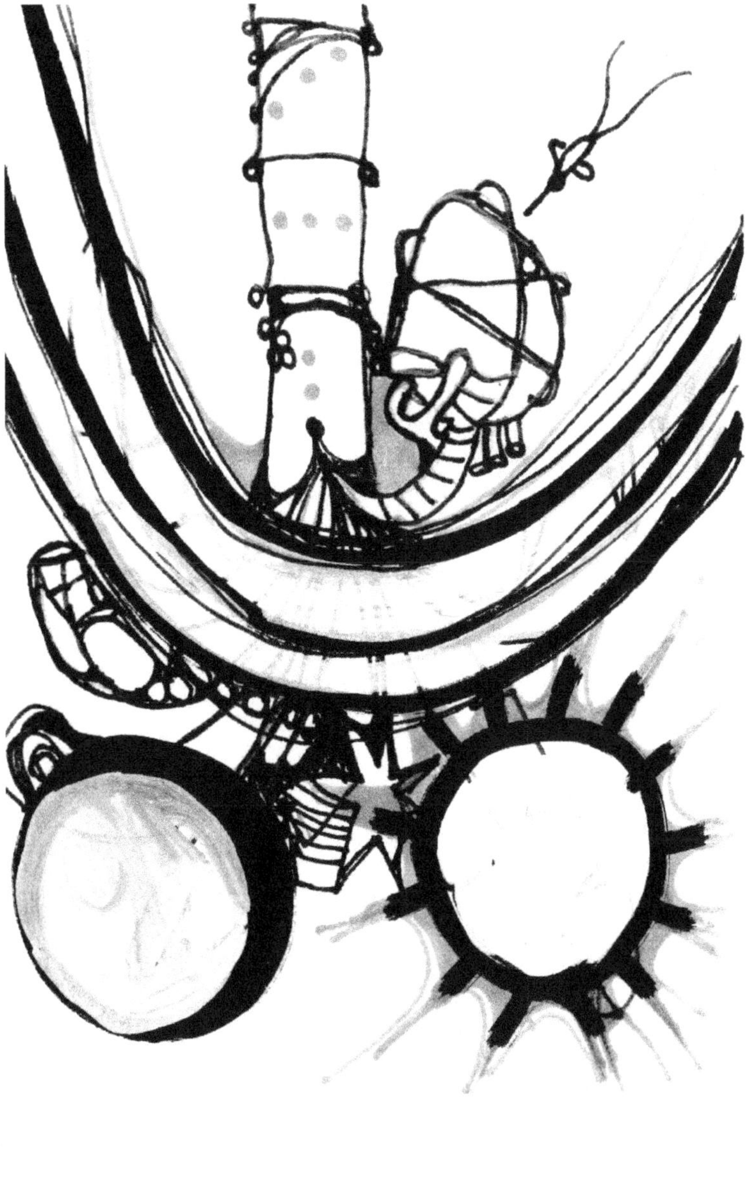

60.

To lead with care and compassion
Is to be in tune with The Source.
In tune with The Source,
There is no space for evil.
Where evil is absent,
little harm can be done.
Peace and Order prevail.
Peace and Order beget Virtue
Bringing all closer to The Source.

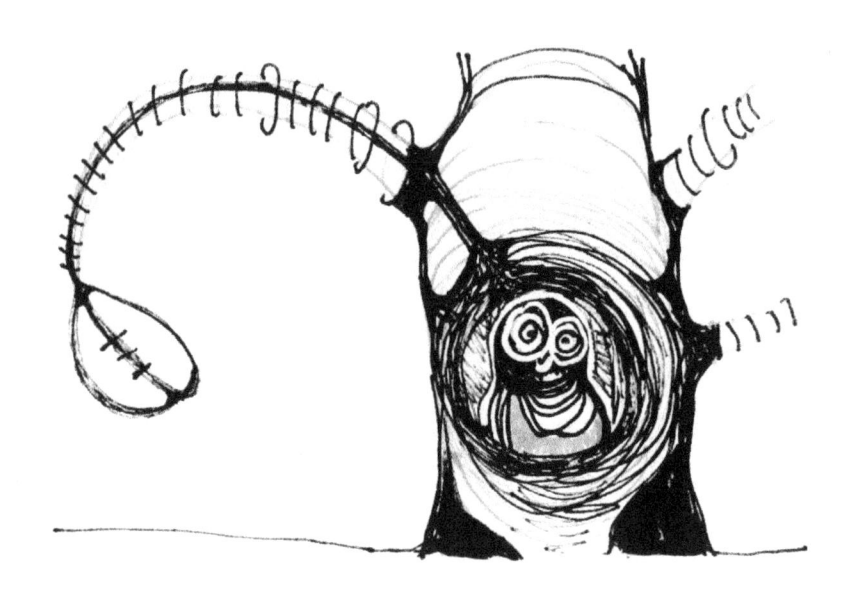

61.

To be humble, is to be in tune with
The maternal genesis that gives life
to all the Universe.

With stillness, The Mother guides.
Both large and small.
Where the small and the large are humble,
All conquer.
All win.
When all win, the Universe is at peace.
When the Universe is at peace,
We are all one people,
All children of the Maternal Source.

62.

All things are born from The Source.
The Good and The Bad.
The good man and the bad man are inextricably linked.
Both born from The One Source.
Treat them both with compassion.
Grant them both forgiveness.
Compassion and Forgiveness
will be your just reward
and lead you to the loving embrace
of The Source.

Find direction in the still of the moment.
Engage the challenges of life, in the quiet of meditation.
Savour the sweetness of the unsweetened air.
Envision the might of simple things.
Let care be the response to bitterness.
Seek simplicity in the seemingly complicated.
Recognise the greatness of the smallest creatures.

Observe how nature does all its work,
simply and with humility.
Manifest in each of Nature's creations
is its omniscience.
   Follow the simple path of Nature.
     Therein is revealed the directions
       to the place of eternal peace,
         the dwelling of The Source.

64.

A mind that is aware from whence it came, is never easily troubled.
It is ever at peace, whilst brittle things and brittle minds
shatter and scatter all around it.
A mind that is aware from whence it came, anticipates danger.
Expectant of everything, nothing injurious occurs.
To know that the widest tree began as a sapling,
To know that the palace is rooted in the earth,
is the beginning of the journey of Humility.
On the Journey, with humility, one accepts inaction.
On the Journey, with humility, one lets go.
Loss and defeat are not possible with inaction.
On letting go, the journey is along a course of acceptance.
With humility, the beginning, the end, and all in between are one and inseparable,
Devoid of success.
Devoid of failure.
Filled with the peace that is the eternal gift of The Source.

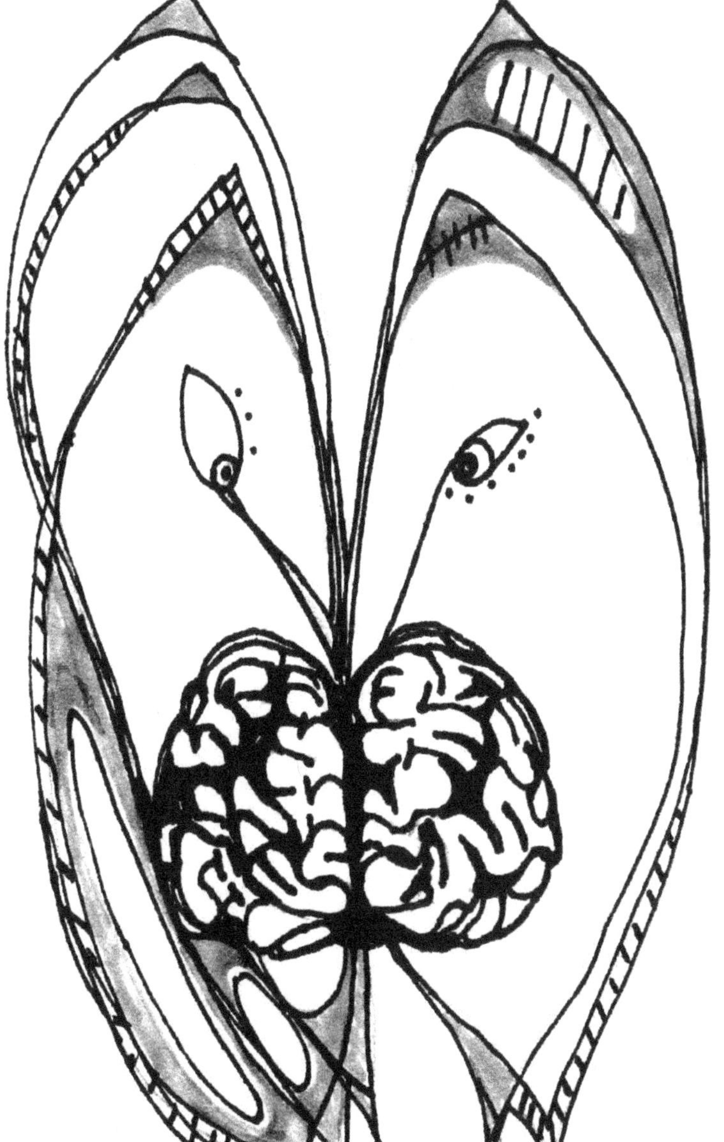

65.

Those who think they know
seek to hoard knowledge as power.
They withhold, in the hope
that those who know they
do not know, will forever
remain in darkness.
Alas, the knowledge of life
Is revealed to all,
through death.
The clever wielder of powers
cheat themselves,
whilst they attempt to cheat
the people.
In the end Virtue and Wisdom
intertwine and deliver all
back to The Source.

The rivers run to the sea, becoming one with the Eternal Water.

Eternal Water, Master of all flows.

We walk the earth, inevitably to become a particle of the Eternal Terrain.

Eternal Terrain, Master of all flesh.

Eternal Water, Eternal Terrain.

They guide all with humility.

Never in competition, always in harmony

ever knowing that The Source is the one Eternal Guide.

67.

All beings, all things, acknowledge The Source.
No being, nothing compares to The Source.
Ever knowing, yet unknown to all beings and all things,
The Source endures.
Three treasures are bestowed upon those
who earnestly seek The Source.
Mercy, Providence, and Empathy.
Courage is born of Mercy.
Providence yields Generosity.
Enlightened Leadership is born of Empathy.
In the pursuit of self-aggrandisement,
Mercy is discarded and bravery lauded.
Unyielding, generosity is stifled and greed celebrated.
Empathy suppressed, the ego flourishes,
And all beings die a thousand deaths.
Through it all, the incomparable Mercy of The Source endures.
Keeping the Heavens eternally safe.

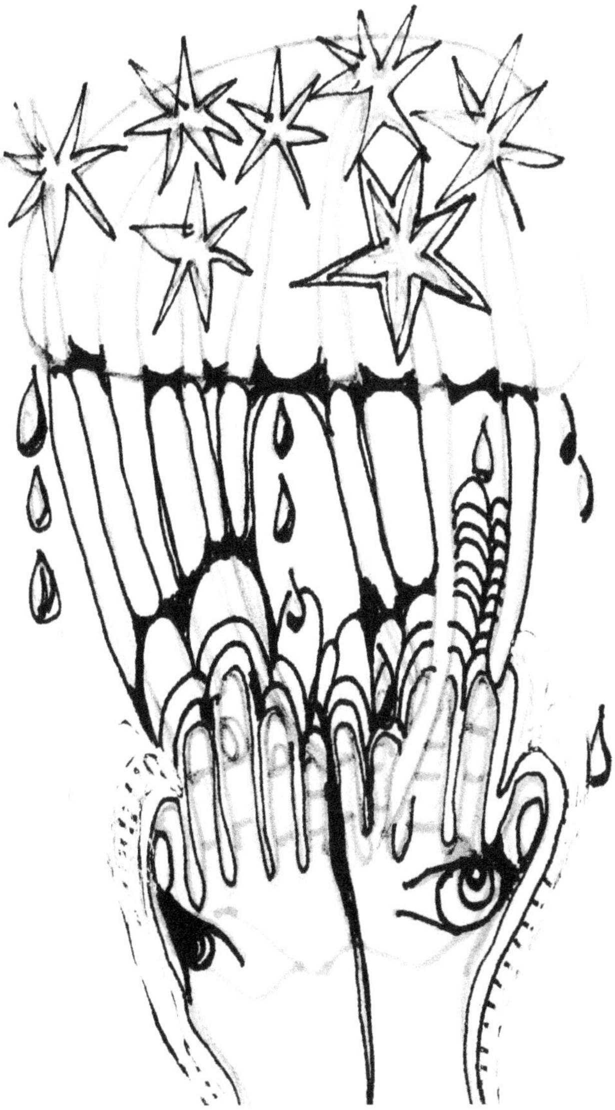

68.

Tranquility is the hallmark of the good soldier.
Calm is the hallmark of a good fighter.
Forgiveness is the hallmark of the good winner.
Humility is the hallmark of a good employer.
Where there is good there is little striving
And Virtue flourishes.
Where there is Virtue, there is Harmony .
Harmony is the bridge that brings all beings
To unity with The Source.

If we both don't make the first move,
there is little likelihood of conflict.
If we both give a little,
there is room for compromise.
To do so is to both win and lose.
To both win and lose,
is to value the other's strength as equal to our own.
To fight to win, ultimately, is to lose.

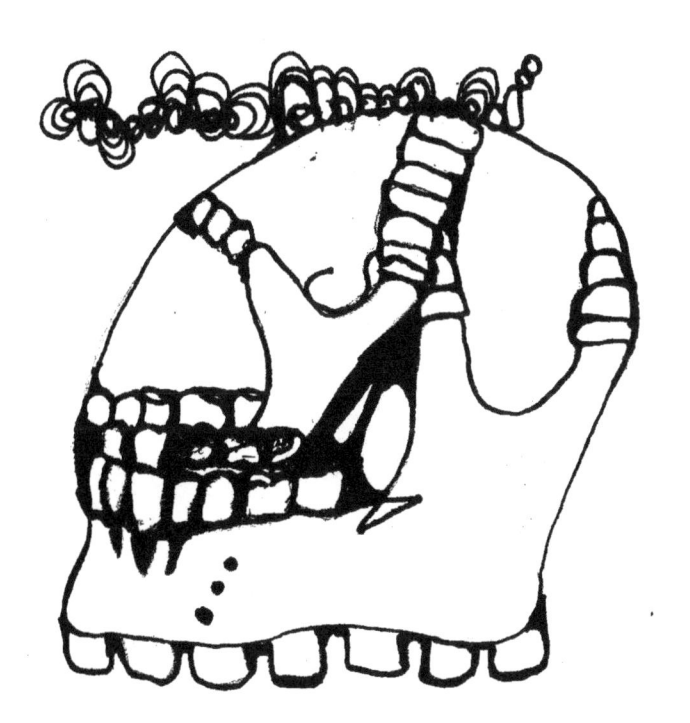

70.

The message of The Sage is simple.
It is universal.
All can hear it and share it.
If they choose.
The message is Love.
From the beginning of time
Love has been the message of The Sage
He shares it with all beings.
The Sage is the medium of The Source,
The Fountain of Love.

To know that one does not know all,
is the strength given by humility.
To not know that one does not know all,
is the weakness inflicted by the ego.
To renounce the ego is to be humble.
Being humble, one follows the path of The Sage.
Following the path of The Sage unites one with The Eternal Source.

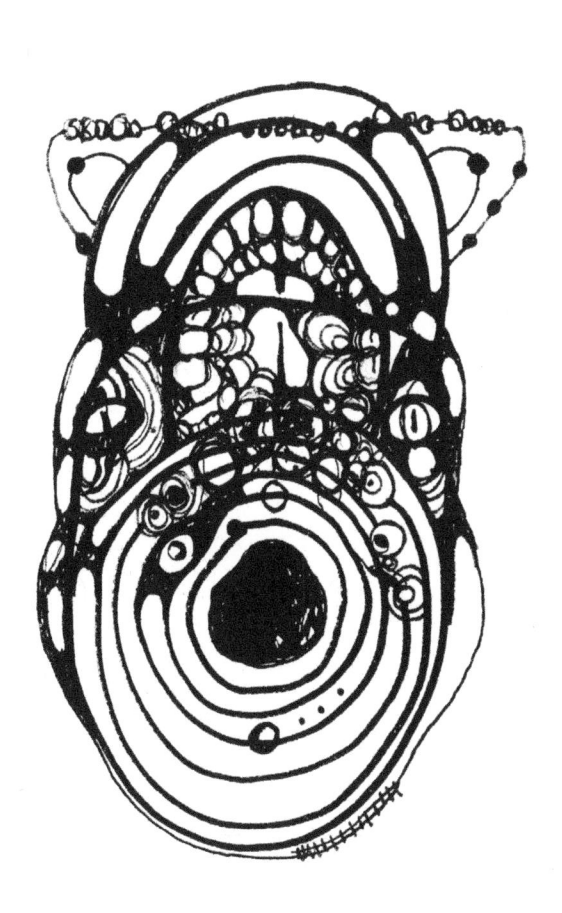

72.

Arrogance, the crown of the egotist,
is the cause of distress for all who cross his path.
It is better not to work with him.
It is safer not to cohabit with him.
He is best left to massage his own ego.
Humility is the Crown of the Sage.
Men who follow him have self-respect.
They are humble.
To work with them is ever pleasurable.
To cohabit with them is ever desirable.

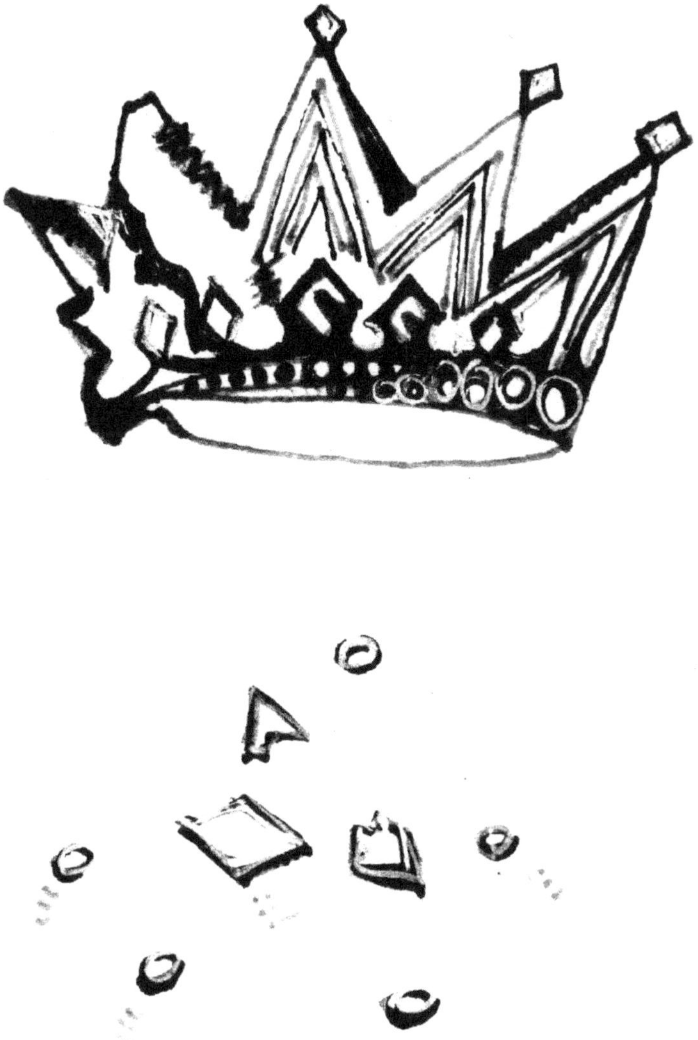

73.

Armed with his ego and bravery, the self-admirer strives for legacy,
in life and in death.
Blessed with humility, the self-effacing strives only to do good.
The Sage acknowledges them both,
one with favour, one less so.
Who knows which is more favoured, which less so?
The Source?
The Source does not speak.
The Source does not strive.
The Source is at ease, never wanting, its needs always met.
It encompasses the universe and brings everything to the state of everlasting peace,
Ultimately.

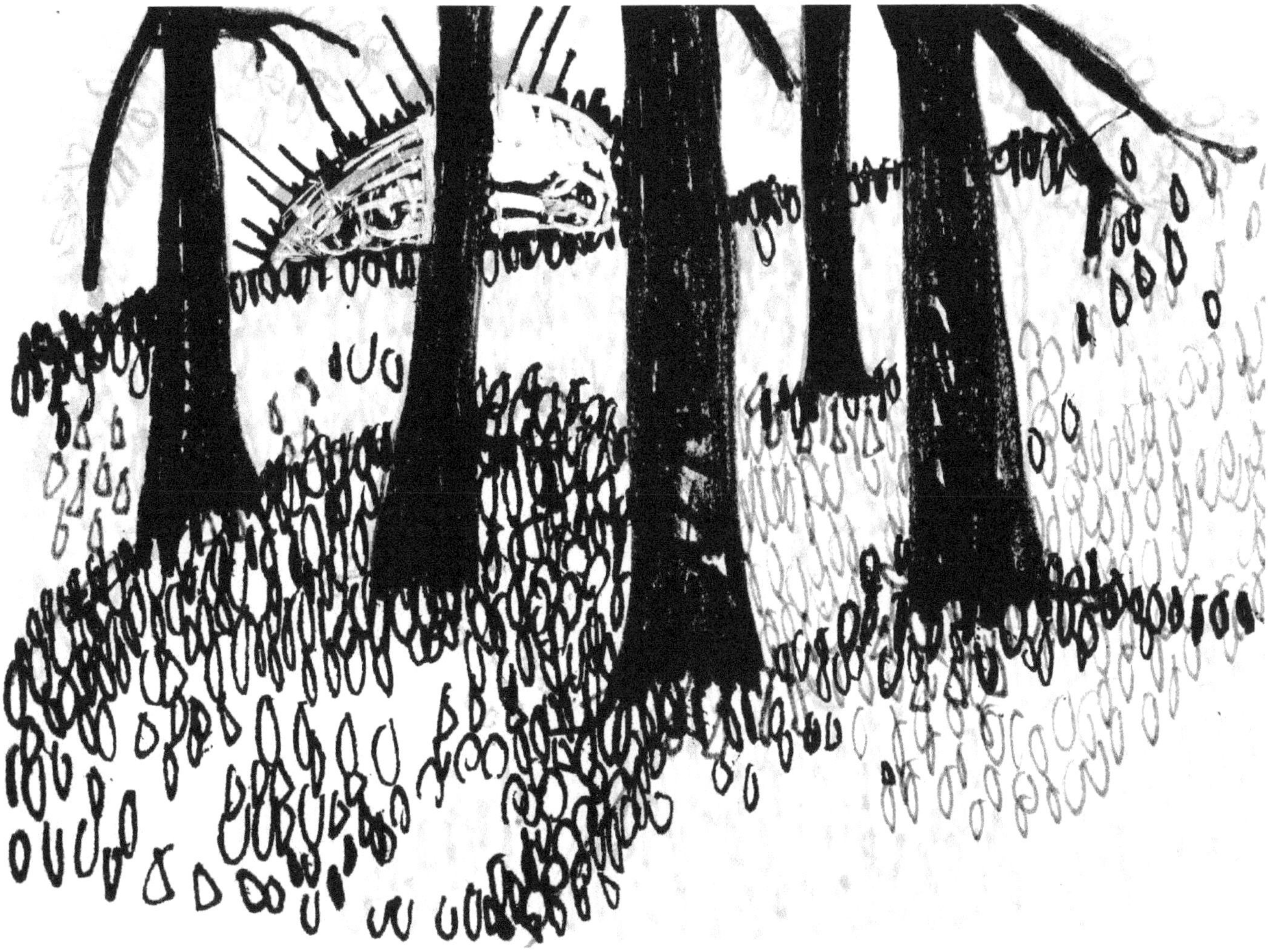

74.

To know no fear of death, is to know fear in living.
To live in fear of death, is to know death interminably.
Fear of death is self-execution.
Usurping the role of the executioner
Is to deny the infinite wisdom and love of The Source.

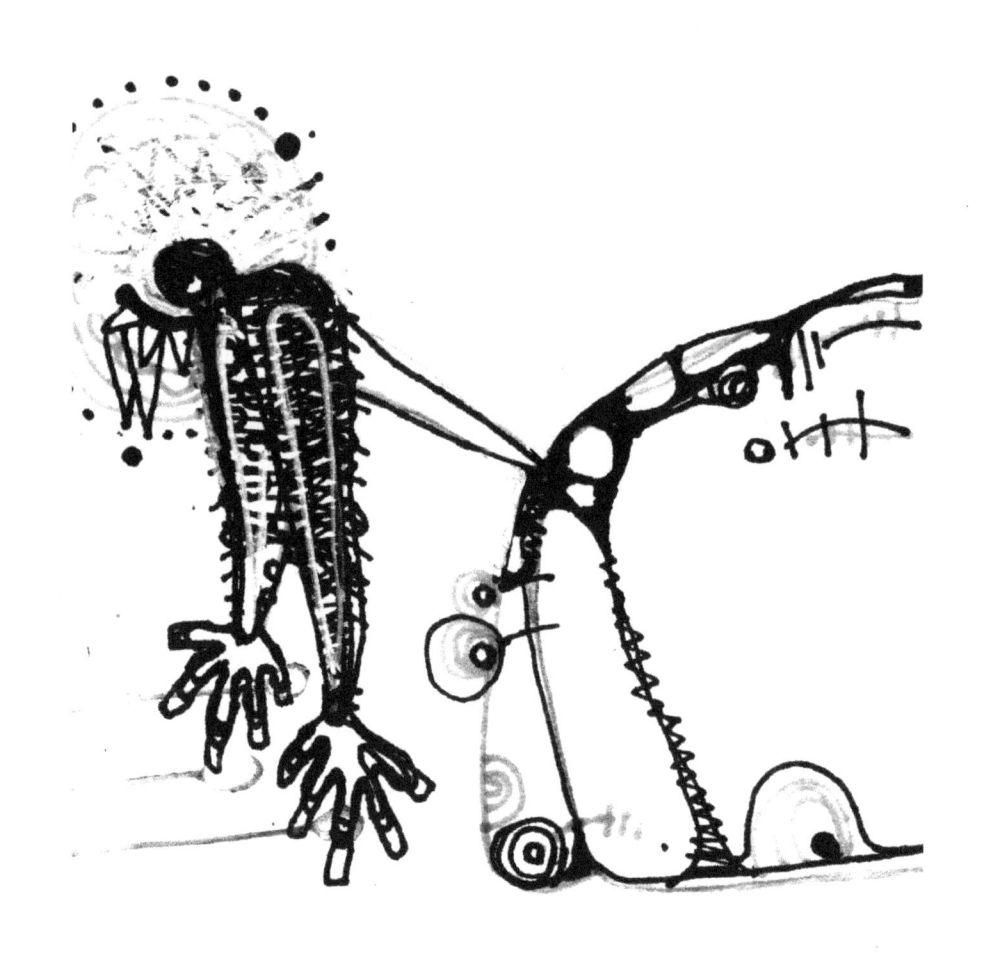

75.

The rulers and the wealthy arrange
for wealth to be concentrated in their hands.
The people are left in dire need.
Insatiable greed and dire need breed rebellion.
In need, life has little value,
with greed, life has little meaning.

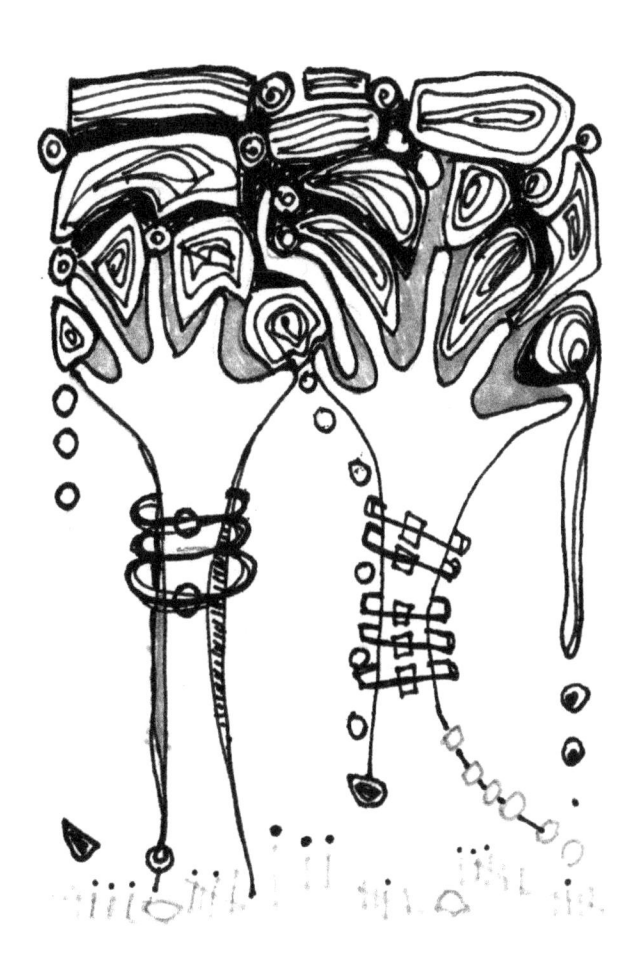

76.

At birth, one is gentle, one is innocent.
Everyone is in need of help.
In death, one is rigid, one has sinned.
Everyone is beyond the need for help.
Rigidity and Sin, the hallmarks of the living dead.
Gentleness and Compromise nurture the living.
Without flexibility, the battle of life is lost.
Rigidity and arrogance portend failure.
Accommodation and tenderness ensure victory,
over death.

In search of the path of Virtue,
the humble accept the prevailing circumstances.
They value the art of compromise.
In search of the path of Virtue,
the humble assist the poor and less able.
In search of self, one extracts from others.
From the poor and less able more
In search of self, one never knows enough.
The Virtuous Source knows there is enough for all,
having given the bounty of life to all, for all to share.
Silently he observes the self-absorbed.
Silently he assigns them to the nothingness of Eternity.

78.

Like water, kindness, and humility
will overcome the hardness of the heart.
Kindness and humility enrich the human spirit.
Whilst all know it, few are willing to be like water.
And so, The Sage implores the leaders,
to show empathy to the weak,
to embrace the suffering of the poor,
to be vulnerable,
to be like water
to be strong
because you are soft.

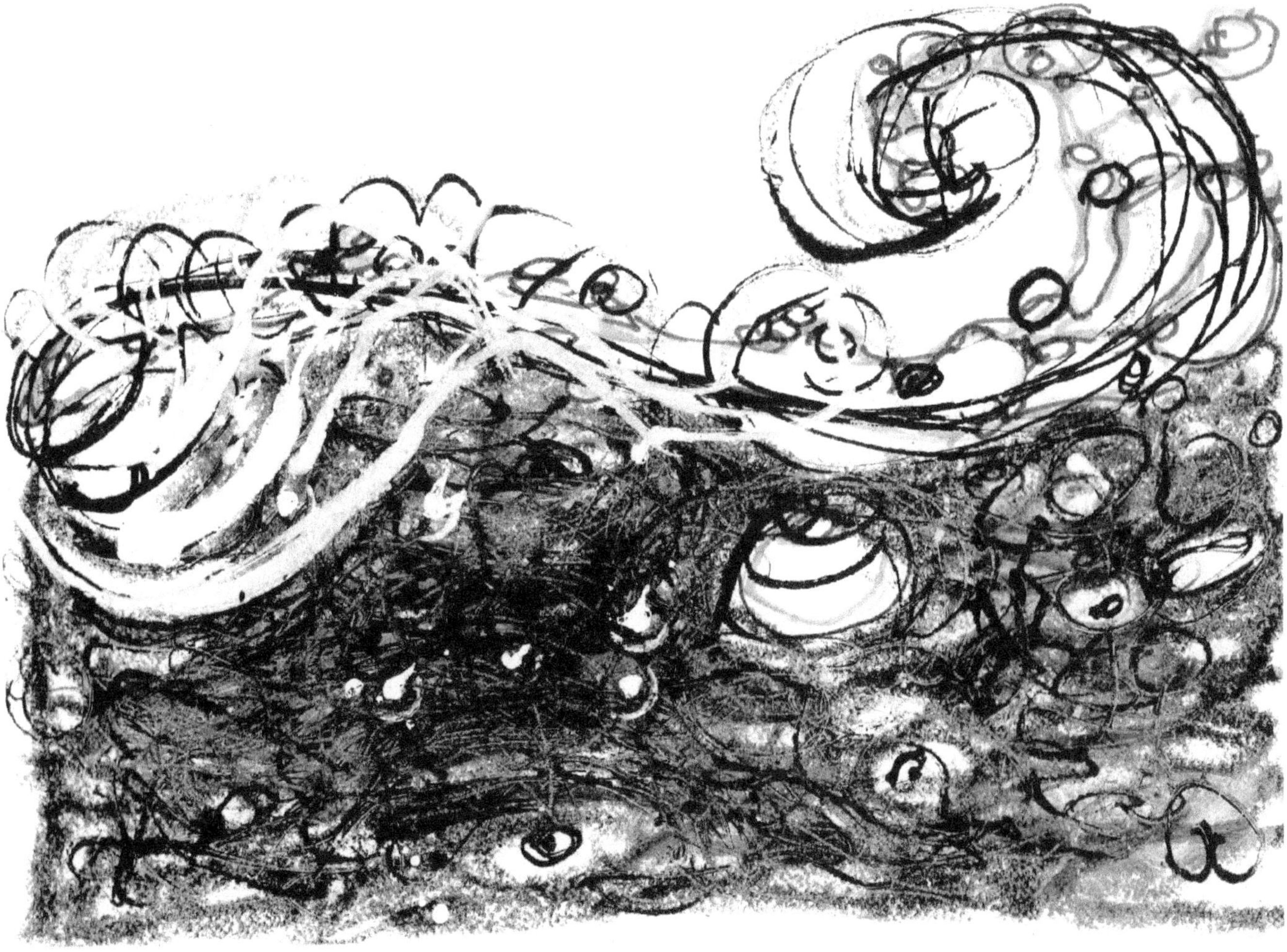

79.

Where conflict arises, seeds of bitterness are planted.
How do the virtuous arrest their growth?
By compromise.
Like The Sage,
the Virtuous few offer their hand in reconciliation.
The many, they seek to exact their pound of flesh.
Meanwhile, The Source looks on impartially,
Knowing that Virtue always will prevail.

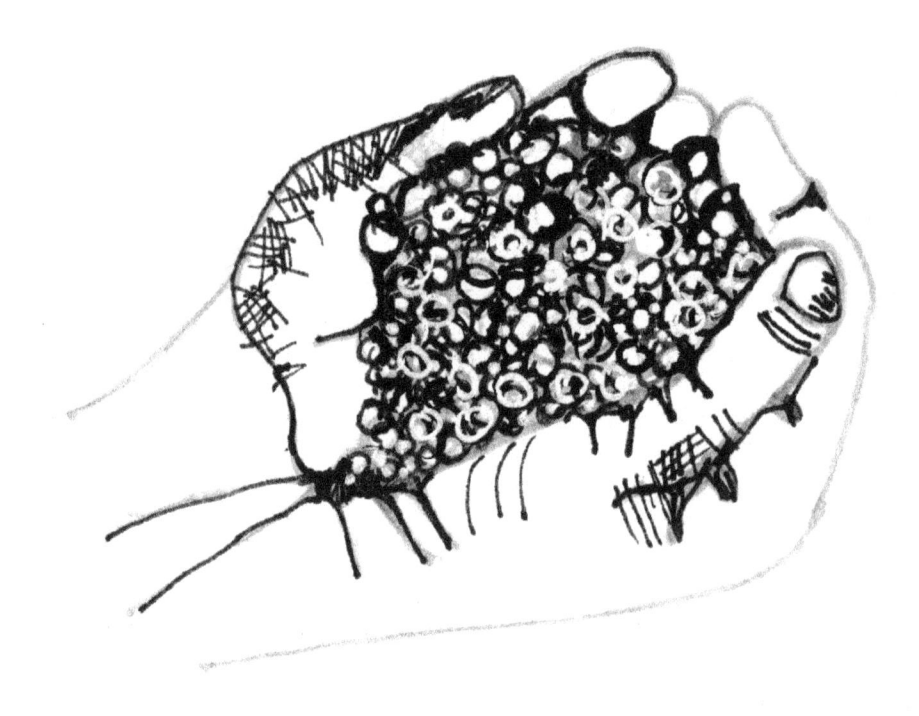

The small country has the benefit of fewer people.
Together they can work more easily for the common good.
Their lives are simple.
Their needs are modest.
Their health and happiness are assured,
once they live in harmony with the other creations of The Source.
At peace, they live in quiet anticipation of the ultimate call,
The uniting with The Eternal Source.

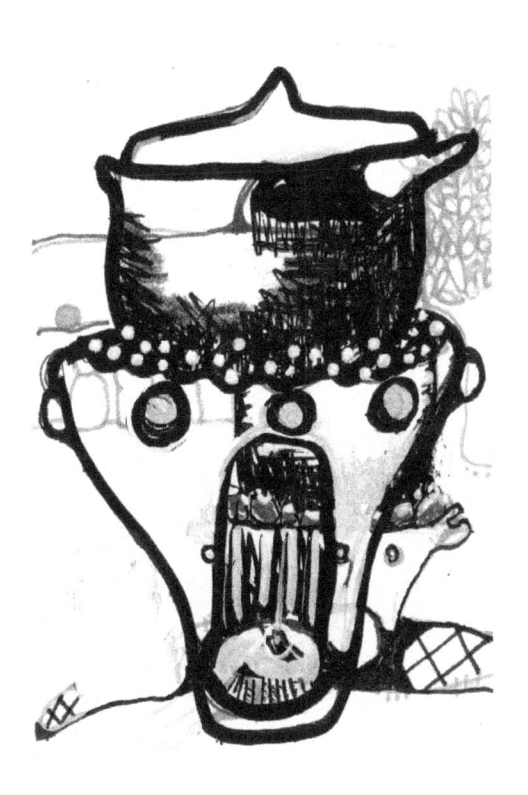

81.

The truth is not always painless,
Painless words are seldom the truth.
The virtuous ones are never argumentative.
The argumentative ones lack virtue.
Knowledge seldom resides with the learned.
It is the unlearned who possess true knowledge.
The Sage is a giver.
In his giving, he reaps bounteous rewards.
The more he gives, the greater his rewards.
The Tao of The Heavens is harmless to all.
The Tao of The Sage is effortless labour.

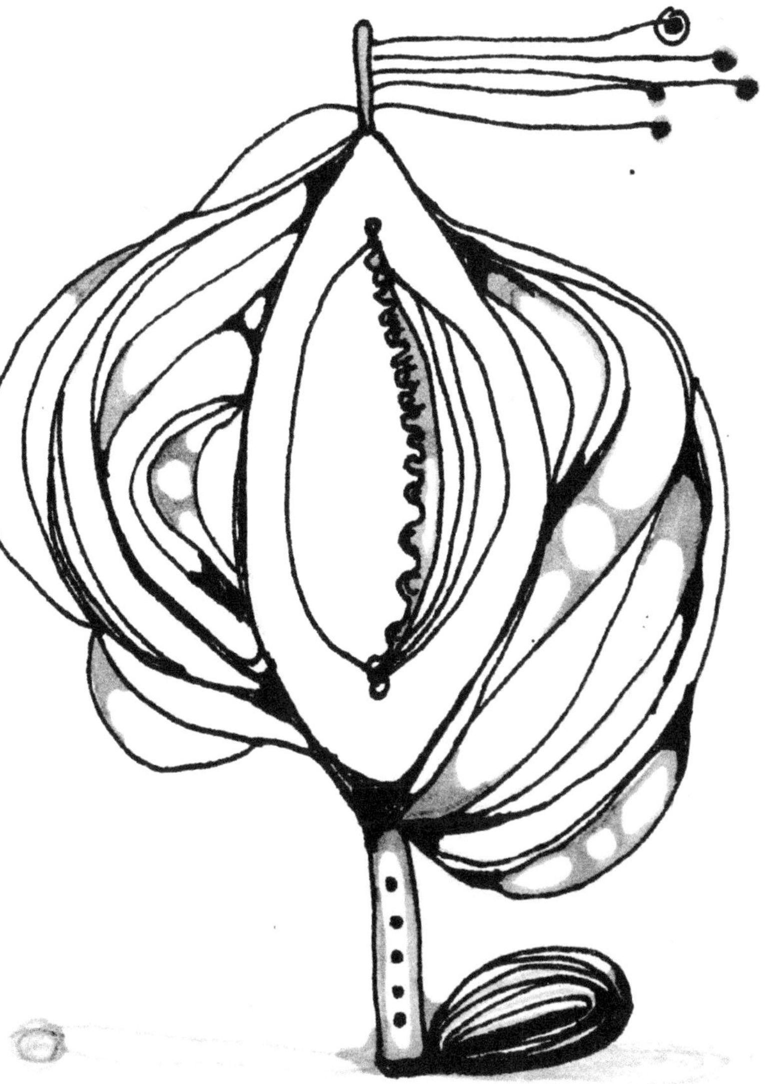

Milton Keynes UK
Ingram Content Group UK Ltd.
UKHW050633220424
441462UK00004B/71

9 798989 740611